Thinking in Jewish

N20

Hank Lazer

Lavender Ink

Thinking in Jewish (N20) by Hank Lazer

Printed in the U.S.A.
First Printing
10 9 8 7 6 5 4 3 2 1   17 18 19 20 21 22
Cover art: Detail from tapestry "Alefbet, Part 3" by Grisha Bruskin.

Book design: Bill Lavender
Library of Congress Control Number: 2017947118
Lazer, Hank
Thinking in Jewish (N20) / Hank Lazer
p. cm.
ISBN: 978-1-944884-27-7 (pbk.)

Lavender Ink
New Orleans
lavenderink.org

Acknowledgments

Thanks for the following editors & publications for publishing many of the poems in *Thinking in Jewish.* The author is grateful for your support. And apologies from the author to any editors & journals that I forgot to acknowledge.

Lana Turner (Calvin Bedient), *EOAGH* (special issued edited by Susan Schultz), *Poets.org* (Academy of American Poets), *Marsh Hawk Review* (Thomas Fink), *1913: a journal of forms* (Sandra Doller), *Plume* (Daniel Lawless), and *La Noria* (Santiago, Cuba; Oscar Cruz).

And thanks, as well, to Greg Randall for his invaluable assistance.

Cover image: detail from *Alefbet* (tapestry), Grisha Bruskin, copyright by the artist. Used by permission of Grisha Bruskin, with thanks to the Meyerovich Gallery, San Francisco, www.meyerovich.com, for providing the image.

for Jake Marmer

2/12/11

"It takes a while to settle into the pages of the book
to settle into the being of the book it takes
an odd kind of leisure

hours a winter morning before anyone else is awake
ice slowly melting on the dead
hydrangea blooms

"We understand that shapes or forms pass into and out of being, while something endures." <67>

hours to under
stand when each word is transit transitory door
way each word attended to surpassing understanding a winter morning

"... the there is, which wounds less than disappearance does." <70>

2/13/11

in the final book hard bound slow writing thinking to make contribute a shape fit for the passing a passing a small death a foretaste so one concludes i.e. something is over

3/1/11

"There is no pure being, then, nothing to think." <74>

don't worry, it's nothing

"Nothingness

runs

through

being."

<75>

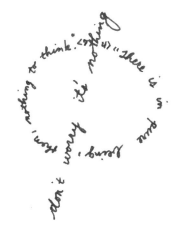

3/4/11

don't worry   it is nothing

as it so happens what i am when i am thinking or writing

don't worry   it is nothing

"Pure being is in fact nothing, neither
more nor less
than nothing." <74>

don't worry   it is nothing

first of the finches first bluebirds nesting humid stormy
front moving through

don't worry   it is nothing

"A nothingness that is obtained not by pure abstraction

don't worry   it is nothing

but as a kind of seizure.

don't worry   it is nothing

In death, one does not make an abstraction of being—

don't worry   it is nothing

it is of us that an abstraction is made." <78>

don't worry really it is nothing

3/6/11

one

two

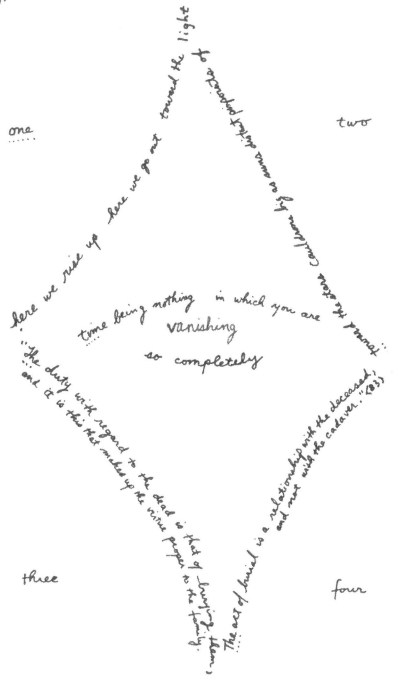

here we rise up here we go out toward the light

of extinct pinpricks as big as cauldrons the stars toward:

time being nothing in which you are

vanishing

so completely

"The duty with regard to the dead is that of burying them,

and it is this that makes up the virtue proper to the living.

The act of burial is a relationship with the deceased,

and not with the cadaver." (83)

three

four

as that had been the way foretold
as we thought & wrote about
made as it were or came into vision
a great spiral jetty
a fundamental shape
made of time a place
in which we could turn into
& after a time
we no longer could see it
though we continued to turn as foretold
within the vanished shape
& having lost sight of it for a time
it came back into our vision
we arose
exactly as we were vanishing as we were turning
into

from another shoreline of g-d who comes to mind
"Everything is fulfilled, everything is consummated
when one is dead.... with death, he who had been a consciousness
is now submitted to matter, that matter has become
the master of a being that was formed, that was a self-consciousness.
One does not want this conscious being to be given over to matter, ...

the appearance of nature's domination over the one who had been conscious
must be rendered invisible."
<85>

3/8/11

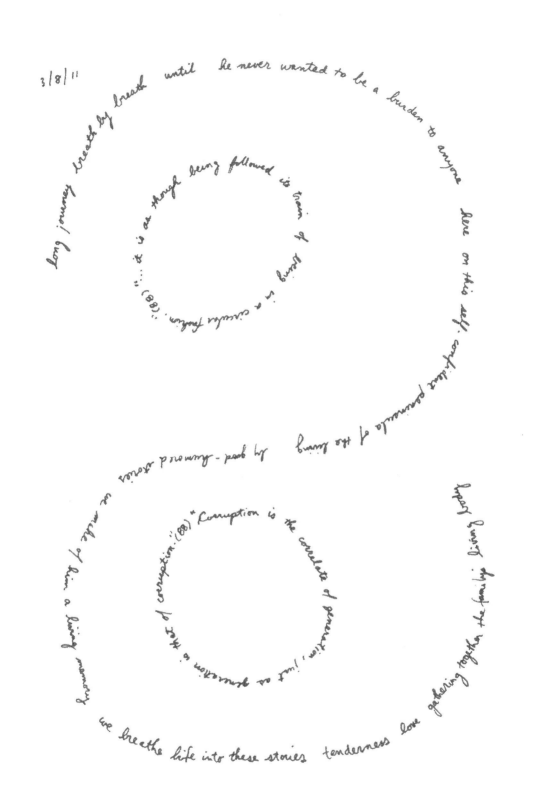

long journey breath by breath until he never wanted to be a burden to anyone here on this self-confident peninsula of the living by word-of-mouth stories we make of him a living memory

"...it is as though being followed is train of thought being is a circular fashion." (88)

we breathe life into these stories tenderness love gathering together the family living legacy

"Corruption is the correlate of generation; just as generation is that of corruption." (88)

gold

finch

& then

another

at the thistle

feeder

*

the breathing tube goes down his throat & into his lungs
& the respirator does the breathing for him. he is sedated.

*

"Does
death not
imply a rupture with
the comprehension of being?... Death is
the end of what makes the thinkable thinkable, and
it is in this sense that it is unthinkable.... This end finds no model in

intelligibility."
(90-91)

3/14/11

i saw his last breath drew an entire community into that mystery

his work is done

we have work to do

"Time is pure hope. It is even the birthplace of hope." <96>

musical

it is also what makes him think moving through

had to say some had been said in the dream some had a final life

in the region of the possible where we think we

"y'all need to cut y'all's lights on bright"

spoke it & spoke it only once said what the spirit

in thinking in conversation

"the fear of dying is the fear of leaving a work unfinished." <101>

four
nights before
you died your daughter
woke up at two in the morning
a coldness passing through her body
a chill i: she awoke saying or hearing
psalm twenty-three though i walk through the valley
of the shadow of death deep of the valley or

we knew him

it felt as if

you never know people you come

" instants

infinite strands
of interesting time

go by as rumbling
a distant thunderhead
drawn out

the life of the scribe
passed on to the son
though they were things" 1083

the oxygen tubes down the nasal passageway
had made it impossible for the ICU attendants to shave
under his nose so when the mortician got the body he very
carefully groomed the moustache good thing his daughters
looked in the day before the funeral i told the mortician no he never had facial hair do
something ; so the mortician shaved off the moustache

3/16/11

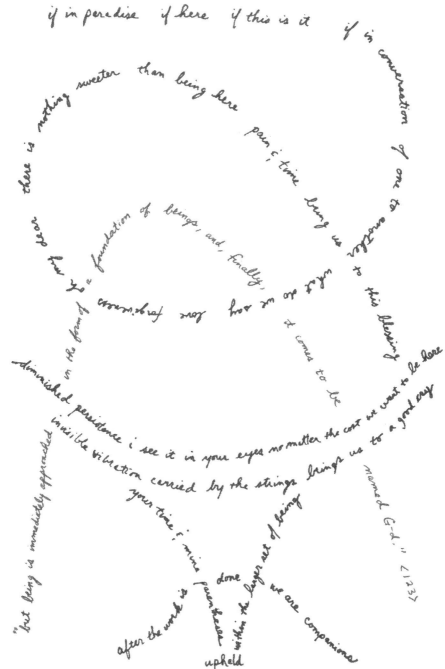

if in paradise if here if this is it

if in conversation of one to another to this blessing

there is nothing sweeter than being here

pain & time bring us

what do we say love forgiveness of how dear

in the form of a foundation of beings, and, finally, it comes to be

diminished persistence i see it in your eyes no matter the cost we want to be here

invisible vibration carried by the strings brings us to a good way

your time & mine

after the work is done

parentheses

upheld

within the larger act of being

we are companions

"but being is immediately approached named G-d." <1237

3/18/11

many books within the book as for being as for time there could be no likeness of them each ; every is a likeness of known knowing all at once ; it continues whether we think about it or not as words held inward sound enumeration ; as the cause to know it to imagine she gave birth to it as the loyal dog is so happy upon your return as you • knowing how happily the echoes the pain your aware to say it a thing it for a moment to awaken

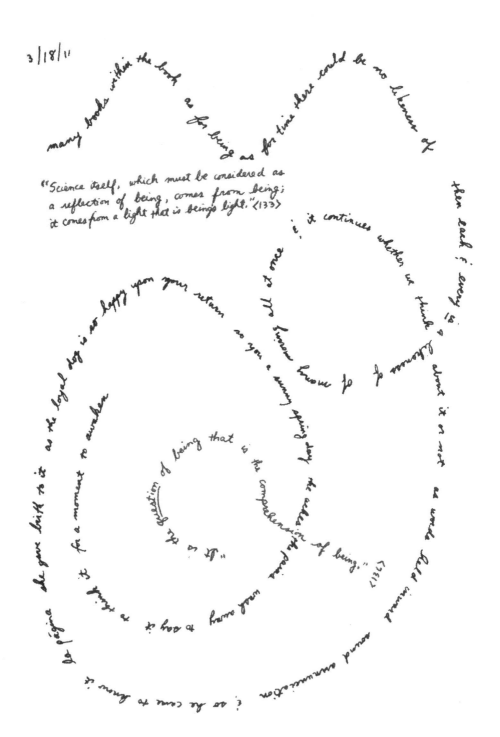

"Science itself, which must be considered as a reflection of being, comes from being; it comes from a light that is being's light." ‹133›

"It is the question of being that is the comprehension of being." ‹136›

3/19/11

the dead become eternal we stand beside them still / who is crying over what's what is he / saying the flowers look lovely let we turn away

with eyes closed

can you see it

by means of hearing

we are this close to one another

when asked his widow says NO

he died at 90 so alive

uncanny sense

i know it all will end

"in the verb 'to be,' which grammarians too lightly call 'auxiliary.'" <129>

"to think of language as a question" <128>

"Behind everything that we do, is this repose." <130>

3/20/11

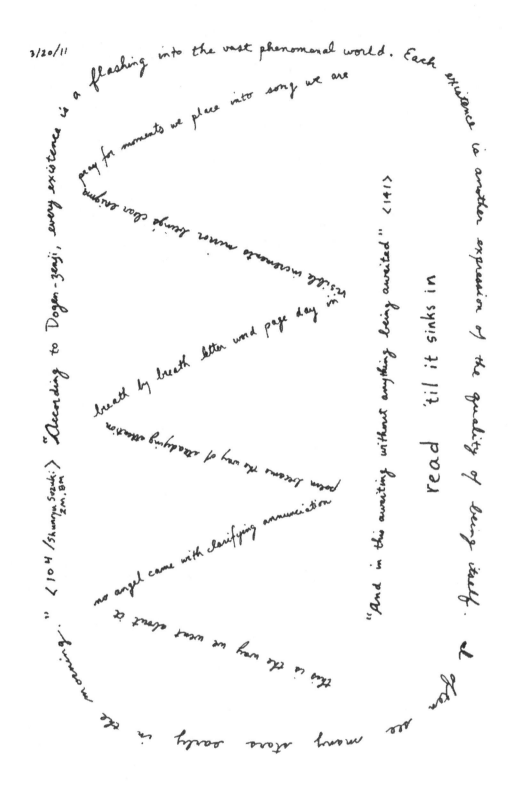

"According to Dogen-zenji, every existence is a flashing into the vast phenomenal world. Each existence is another expression of the quality of being itself. & often see many stars early in the morning." <104 / Shunryu Suzuki: ZM, BM>

this is the way we went about it
no angel came with clarifying annunciation
poem becomes the way of steadying attention
breath by breath letter word page day
visible increments mirror being's clear enigma
pray for moments we place into song we are

"And in this awaiting without anything being awaited" <141>

read 'til it sinks in

3/25/11

hello, earthlings   we come in peace

"Let us take up the question again: can
we think of G-d outside of onto-theo-logy,
outside of G-d's reference to being?
To articulate this question, we are
going to look for forms of
thought different from
intentionality, that
is, forms of
thought
solicited
wakefulness a tic in steady being
by what
overflows
them. Thus the
Kantian ideas are
forms of thinking that
overflow knowledge and
point toward a subjectivity
awakened by what it could not contain." <149>

fire fly

hello, earthlings   we come in peace

3/27/11

round is round
reading around
one day one morning
a gray day
crepe myrtle putting forth fair leaves of spring
dogwood beginning to bloom
sounds of a possible storm
rocking around
if you come across it
a passage
everything changes
i am still
in motion
i am still
in motion
but for how long

"and this intelligibility
appears paradoxical in that each
term in itself is without meaning, and
they receive their meaning from the way they are
arranged with respect to one another." <150>

the book is the sum of its pages

"There is
something of a
tension in the individual,
at once torn from the whole
and aspiring to that whole." <155>

some of its pages

from one to another

"It is, as the totality of what is,
the supreme concreteness
form of individuality.
and
It is not a thing
(on the contrary, all things
suppose it), and yet
it is "something"

remind me what does this have to do with thinking of g-d

the book is the sum of its pages

that is." <155>

4/3/11

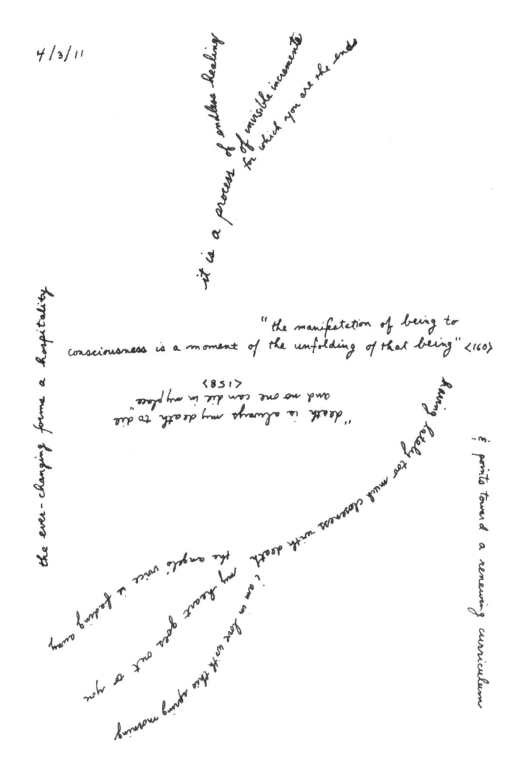

it is a process of endless healing
of invisible increments
for which you are the ends

"the manifestation of being to consciousness is a moment of the unfolding of that being" <160>

"death is always my death to die
and no one can die in my place."
<158>

the ever-changing forms a hospitality

being solely too much closeness with death

the angelic voice is fading away

my heart goes out to you

i am in love with this spring morning

& points toward a renewing curriculum

4/6/11

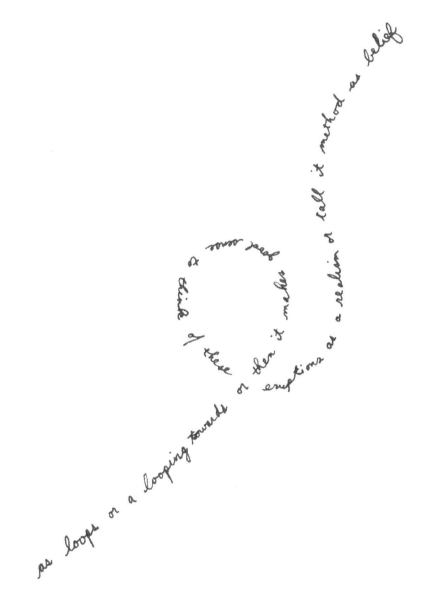

as loops or a looping towards or then it makes feel sense or think of these
eruptions as a relation or call it method as belief

4/8/11

decanter
sings
everyone breathes
thinking

"that all method is belief ... but our poetic content involves relation to an unknown, not a knowledge
or method of it .... 'instead of possession one learns relation.'" (Blaser, 48, 54, 55)

"The gaze is not a finding but a deference. In this way, it is wonder and worship.... And those eyes —
which are found in their innate concreteness, which aim at things and perceive, and which have the name of Lucretius —
learn patience and become an industrious gaze." <164, 165, 166>

"The world is always proportionate
to our knowledge
or to the thought
to which it is always given." <167>

Once
for
each
thing

4/12/11

"In this sense, the empirical world of man's animal nature must be conceived as a bursting of the epic of being, a bursting in which a break, a fissure, or a way out is opened, in the direction of the beyond where a God that is other than the visible gods would abide." <169>

:i: thinking itself is invisible :i:

now has shape

flashes into being

by means of a portal

what upholds

this language ; & resident in it now

& not ours is ours & you fully

4/14/11

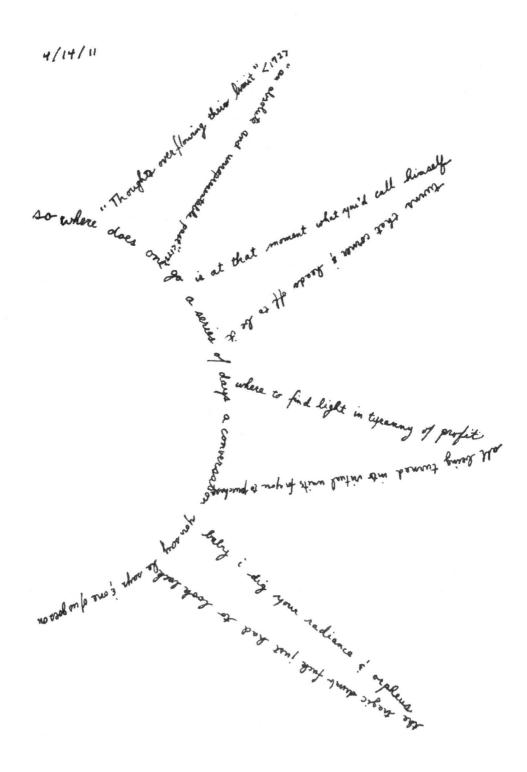

so where "Thoughts overflowing their limit" <1927

"an absolute and unrepeatable position"

so where does one go

is at that moment what you'd call himself

turns that comes & heads off to be it.

a series of days

where to find light in tyranny of profit

a conversation

all being turned into virtual units for you to purchase

you say he says & one of us goes on

baby i dig your radiance & orpheus

the tragic dumb fuck just had to look back

restless

rest
less

restless

rest
less

restless

rest
less

restless

rest
less

restless

rest
less

restless

4/15/11

two different black inks & one blue ink & these have
been the voices given to me as vision kindle kindle
burning bright in ~~flu~~orescence of the night blink

as ever other words are being lived here
these words were always with us "language is
not our own"

here

so you say here the made elaborate way of my
not knowing "as if her mind / sought in me flight
beyond the horizon" returning to strange shape of residence

4/16/11

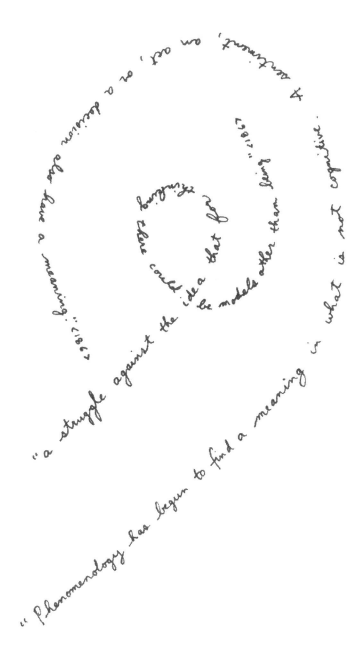

"Phenomenology has begun to find a meaning in what is not cognitive. A sentiment, an act, or a decision also have a meaning." <186>

"a struggle against the idea that for thinking there could be models other than being." <186>

4/23/11
diamond head

dawn over diamond head seven
surfers at the breakline low
tide exposes brown dying coral
sunrise sing we glory as it is

"a correlation and equality between it concerns me and is fulfilled in nearness itself," <193>

what is thought and thinking itself" <195>

" the glory of the infinite, which commands me and encircles me

and yet by my own voice," <197>

it, so move toward it as called   my
mother is losing her sight   a pooling in
the eyes   gradual darkening of her world
she is (we are) confined to the familiar

the arc of seeing persistent thinking of what could be downward to darkness unable to fly

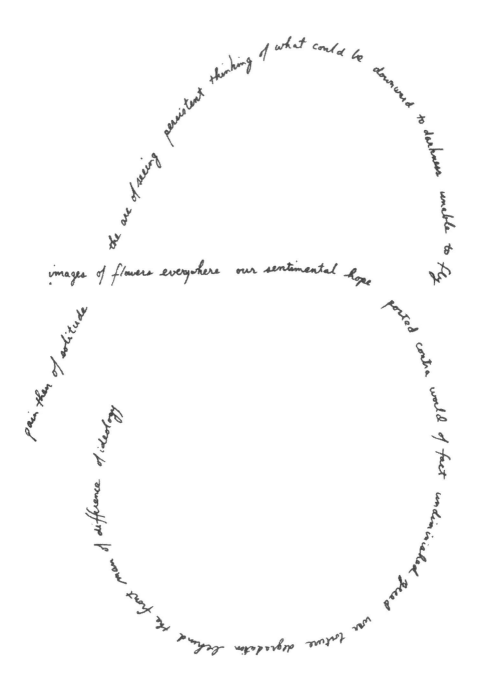

images of flowers everywhere our sentimental hope

posted contra world of fact undiminished good war torture degradation behind the fears mean of difference of ideology

pain then of solitude

at the intersection
of futility &
glory we walk

perimeter of the
park is any
paradise enough where

ever you are
think this one
now in-this

breath the adequate
paradise walking with
deliberation this one

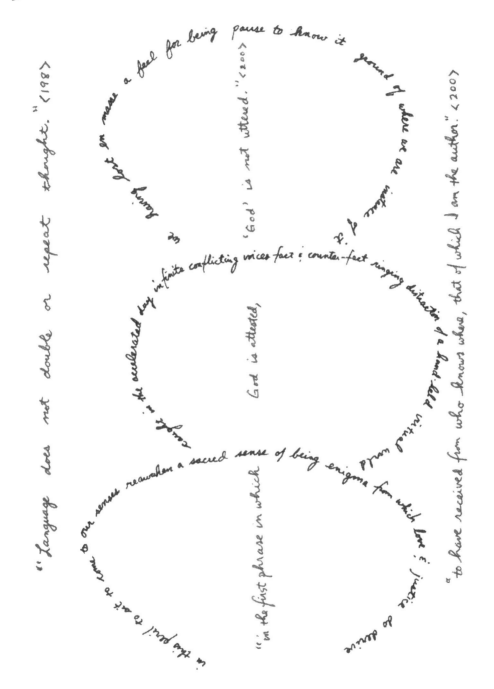

4/24/11
diamond head

"Language does not double or repeat thought." <198>

in this peril to sit to come to our senses reawaken a sacred sense of being enigma from which love & justice do derive

caught in the accelerated day infinite conflicting voices fact & counter-fact ringing distraction of a hand-held virtual world

we having lost en masse a feel for being pause to know it ground of where we are instance of it.

"in the first phrase in which

God is attested,

'God' is not uttered." <200>

"to have received from who knows where, that of which I am the author." <200>

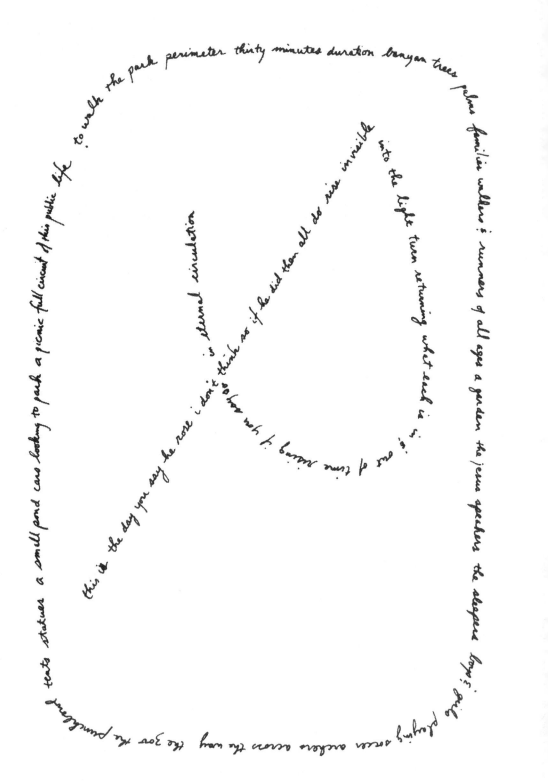

; to walk the park perimeter thirty minutes duration banyan trees palms families walkers ; runners of all ages a garden the jesus speakers the sleepers boys ; girls playing soccer archers across the way the zoo the pineland tents statues a small pond cars looking to park a picnic full circuit of this public life

this is the day you say he rose i don't think as if he did then all do rise invisible into the light turn returning what each is ; is one of time rising if you so

is eternal circulation

4/25/11

privilege

lift the clouds

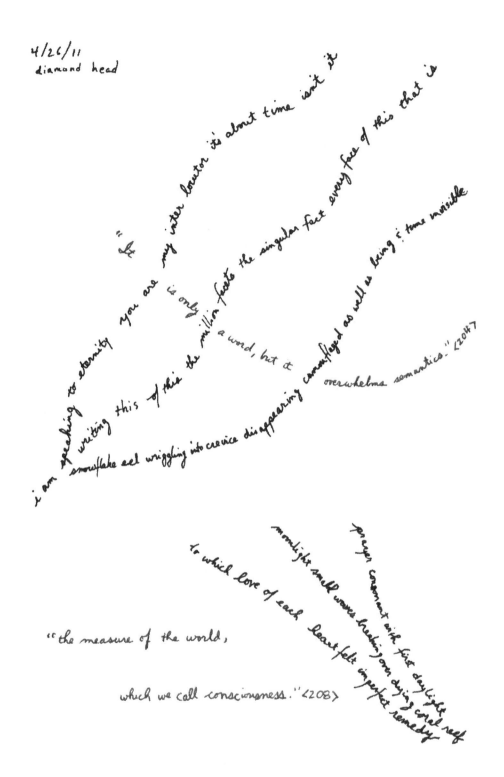

4/26/11
diamond head

i am speaking to eternity you are my inter locutor it's about time isn't it

writing this of this the million facets the singular fact every face of this that is

snowflake eel wriggling into crevice disappearing camouflaged as well as being & time invisible

"it is only

a word, but it

overwhelms semantics." <204>

prayer covenant with first daylight

moonlight small waves breaking over dying coral reef

to which love of each heartfelt imperfect remedy

"the measure of the world,

which we call consciousness." <208>

note

book

magic

notebook

4/30/11
diamond head

swept away to nothingness
remains of a different city

"a bearing witness in which the infinite ... disquiets or awakens the finite" <207>

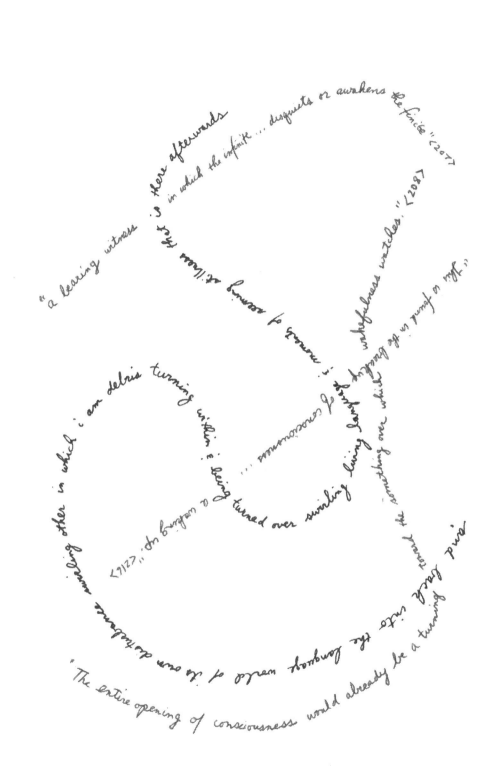

and back into the language world of its own disturbance swirling other in which i am debris turning within i: being turned over swirling living language i: moments of seeming stillness that is there afterwards

toward the something over which wakefulness watches." <208>

"This is found in the breaking up of consciousness ... a waking up." <212>

"The entire opening of consciousness would already be a turning

5/5/11
tuscaloosa
"the infinite
wakes thought up" <220>

the page turns by itself seemingly without wind a breath & the page turns by itself
or by a violent wind a tornado & hundreds of pages are torn & scattered from the book
the funnel in its twisting touches down tearing apart whatever it touches & just beside it
an enigmatic calm as if nothing happened we sit thinking birds return the page turns by itself

" The infinite affects thought and devastates it at the same time;
it affects it in devastating it, and in this way it calls to it." <220>

5/9/11

adonai echad

we are

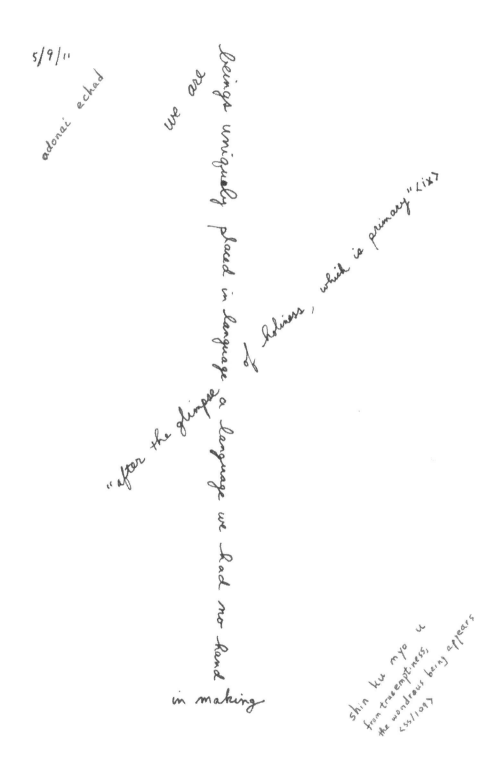

beings uniquely placed in language

of holiness, which is primary" <ix>

"after the glimpse a language we had no hand

in making

shin ku myo u
from trueemptiness,
the wondrous being appears
<55/109>

5/12/11

here a word

as we move among marvels

there a word

5/15/11

coming through the
they are the allies
the voices are coming
of time they are the
the invisible

& so we can we can we know we can

tiptoeing along the edge of the disaster

the voices are
walls of time
of the invisible
through the walls
allies of

5/21/11

"The contemporary world, scientific, technical, and sensualist, sees itself without exit – that is, without God – not because everything there is permitted and, as Dostoyevsky thought, possible, but because everything there is equal. The unknown is immediately made familiar and the new customary." <12>

– so we go to these a-writing – riding where we are sounding – seeing but we are this music thinking O where are we now

"for all the heavenly doors are closed except that through which the tears of the injured pass" <13>

5/28/11

"The fact that reason might be naive and still insufficiently awakened, that it might have to guard against its own assurance" <167>

he would say, 'tell yourself you've got all the time in the world"

"as if… reason that identifies being slept on its feet or walked like a somnambulist, and were still dreaming"

lord knows what

… what exactly

did that mean

contraction of reality

a ground beneath which we find the dead & nothing

6/2/11

call them toward

hope

this kind

of

was

sadly the need of public art to be unobjectionable

if she is susceptible

to learning

Ricœur

"starting from the nonadequation of evidence relative to the

world and to the things therein" <20>

Marcel.

"awakens to itself only

in reflection" <20>

6/8/11
6/10/11

learning to think being
in finding this feeling for being
to being's infinite variations
numbered threads
finity of language & music
still wide awake this morning
of each breath its complex conversion
to finger its many conflicting threads
quietly to yourself

"or the preliminary necessary to awakening" <26> who study
this curriculum of the soul "as if God could abide with-
in me" <26> in the form of our love of the world "as
though the adventure of cognition were not all of the spirituality
of thought, as if it were rather the falling asleep of a wake-
fulness!" <27> witness the energy of attention "rather of
reanimating – or of reactivating – this life" <27> & put on the
prayer shawl "as though consciousness fell asleep in 'being
awakened' to things" <27> yes of course it is here now & now

Such great pleasure in
so musical such pleasure adventure
such is the pleasure in attending
in joy to awaken to the
beginning with the sweet in-
such great pleasure in sitting
in love with the small miracle
this day to wear the prayer shawl
to say it & to sing it

6/11/11

"the astonishing possibility of the sobering up, when the I is liberated from itself and awakens from dogmatic slumber" <29>

"wakefulness arising in the awakening" <28>

Cross Over

"the great flow of being which is god's very mood" <lewis/166> chanting the light of foresight

a brief appearance you have all the time in the world your chance then within this

flow you may be thinking reflecting feeling this moving instance of being : its enduring

emptiness rock in the river you live intimate with it are it strange as language is to you

"a passage from one knowledge to a better knowledge" <29>

"The living of life – an incessant bursting of identification." <30>

6/12/11

"the very spirituality of the spirit remains knowing [savoir]" <29>

"The spirit remains
the presence of being,
of this presence.

"This is an awakening irreducible to knowledge [savoir] and Reason, which does not confine itself to lucidity." <30>

"Music
is a
hidden practice of the soul
which deals in number
without knowing it's so doing; in a
confused perception
the soul
thus achieves that which,
in clearer perceptions,
it is unable to achieve." <RB/357>

founded upon
it is the event
This meaning that,
when it shows itself, cannot but show itself in consciousness, shall not separate itself from the adventure of consciousness which is ontological." <29>

"more contact than the skin can touch" <31>

always at a beginning

6/15/11
Havana

"the anticipation of the future in which humanity, today absent, will exist." <34>

"marxism abandons the heavens to speak the language of the earth." <34>

"understood as hope, humanity is always in advance." <34>

bueno y sin prisa

las tristes maravillas

"The fulfillment of man is the fulfillment of being in its truth." <35>

6/16/11
Havana

some part of being "To posit praxis as conditioning truth is to take time seriously." <37> & so we do now

as we make the real labor in perception slowly labor to know

"Nothing is accessible, nothing shows itself without being determined by the intervention of humans' corporeal labor." <36>

friends here & there each living daily knowing that we have

with a music a thinking that dances with the invisible strange solidarity of our living in language

walking & walking in the extreme beat of this

"what thought is in the course of a life and therefore what art is"

6/17/11
havana 2am
ideas
ideas
ideas
indivisible
(aye)
ideas
ideas
ideas
ideas
invisible
(I)
ideas
ideas
ideas
ideas
ideas
things
(eye)
ideas
ideas
ideas
ideas
ideas
ideas

6/18/11
Ravena

" in which the co-naturality of man and being glimmers as an extreme possibility " <39>

the city: historiador somos juntos in an unspoken hope

" this is his manner of standing in incomplete being " <39>

i will listen to the voices grey day: the steady flow of people through the old city

flow of intimate adjacent just histories a hot cup of strong coffee energy of repair under the watchful eyes of the city: historiador somos juntos in an unspoken hope

if we could learn to be

6/19/11
havana

"caught/ in reality together"

we await their decisions
& we go about our business

who will rise up
of the world peoples
of our world/ kinships

from person to person we build a lasting peace

"the words to be would
already be too much. yet
this is an unformable question

by which is nourished
every other
first question." <40>

the specific void of soul intimation
the word that you alone adore

"Being's coming to itself is certainly impossible
without the end of mourning: of my mourning, and especially the mourning of another." <417>

together
in this
silence

on which

mourning with the humility of creatures who know they barely matter

we rest

6/20/11
havana

a charged field

“Ustedes no son los mismos que dejaron atrás esa estación”
(TSE)

“Physical, economic, and political causes pierce a hole over man as if he were but one natural reality among others.

the situation of human liberty as to the mind. A transcendental subjectivity does not annul the effect which the penetration of

which can have, as a brief point of a revolver bullet, into the heart of the I, which is but viscera.” <43>

a singular thread

as one is among the billion filaments

“the exercise of the activity expressed by the verb of verbs, by the verb to be

which we lightly call auxiliary.” <43>

“considerar el futuro y el pasado con mente semejante”
(TSE)

wait
&
see

7/4/11

Compassion on condition
be like us
do what we say

"that is, the aging that comes about, although no one brings it about" <50>

ride it out never the morning lucidity that there are words that

resume reborn for the young not possible to take the long view of time

we live with them & say them too rapidly to one another

"A patience of awaiting, time is a question, a search, a demand, and a prayer." <50>

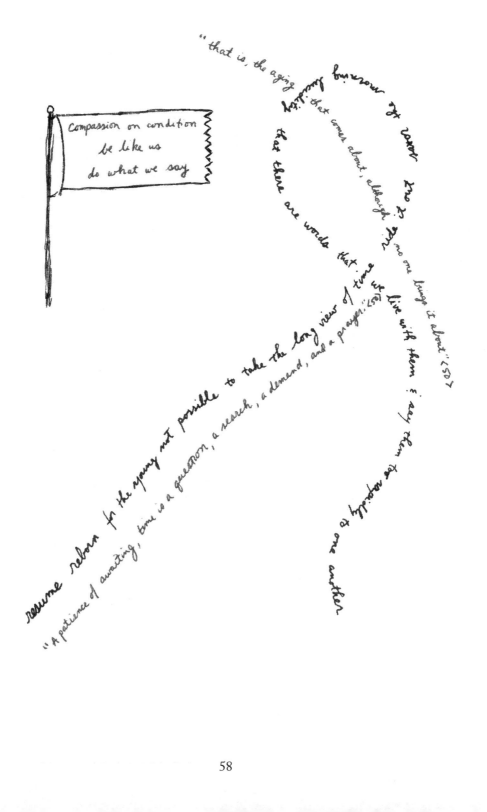

7/10/11

into an 'experience had by a subject'" [60]

to the point of the bursting of presence

"an extreme tension

"It refers to an awakening

It is an attention to..." [60]

watch over being.

but also to a shocking

in the form of lucidity.

& without forethought sweetly in the circle of our sounding & say it & sing &.

to lift up our voices to be uplifted to live

yes yes & yes

oh please go on

to.

7/16/11
London

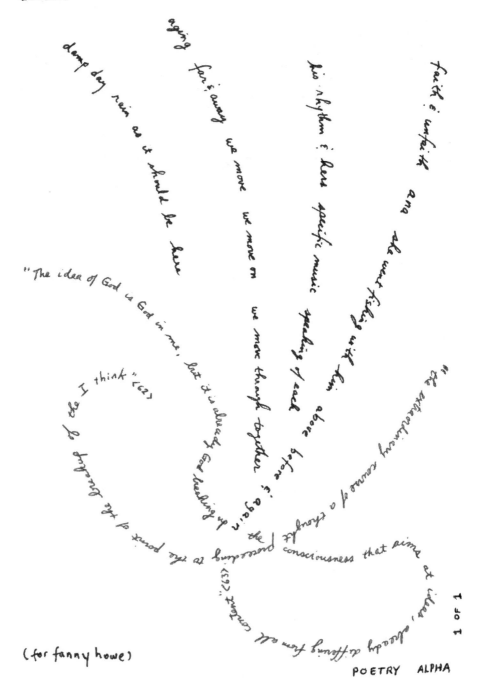

faith & unfaith   and   she went fishing with him   above   before & again

his rhythm & hers   specific music   speaking of each

aging far & away   we move   we move on   we move through together

damp day rain as it should be   here

"The idea of God is God in me, but it is already God breaking up the proceeding to the point of the Breakup of the I think" <62>

"the extraordinary course of a thought consciousness that aims at ideas, already differing from all content" <63>

(for fanny howe)

POETRY ALPHA

7/17/11
London
5:15am

it is time the measured way measure for measure so it goes it's not my thing the best medium do you remember not my thing it's always now i the light is one it is time i meant to say the lightning

as i am one by one two of everything a bewildering collection i thought it is time now your face morning morning

is on the e is silent anyway i am here awake i cannot say your name full measure of how it now comes to mind

yes give this machine a rest
oh my son my only son so good to hear your voice so far away
in this rain the gray machinery of time
this language that they say is mine is not
what am i native to if not the question
a thing which has / which is its own time a questionable being
without announcement
you & i
are
simply here
what else
could we have been
waiting for
nothing
absolutely nothing

< for glenn >

7/18/11
London

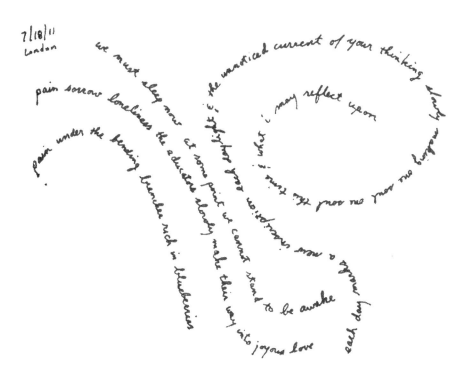

we must sleep now at some point we cannot stand to be awake

pain sorrow loneliness the educators slowly make their way into joyous love

pain under the bending branches rich in blueberries

each day requires a new inscription: good thinking it is the unnoticed current of your thinking slowly wading on and on and the time: what i may reflect upon

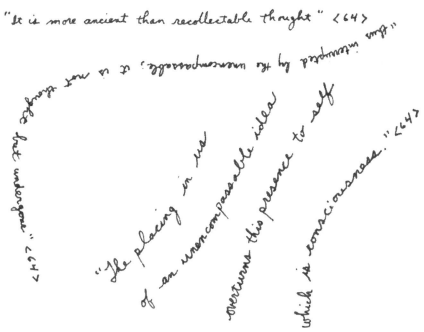

"It is more ancient than recollectable thought" <64>

"thus interrupted by the unencompassable: it is not thought but undergone." <64>

"The placing in me
of an unencompassable idea
overturns this presence to self
which is consciousness." <64>

7/23/11
Edinburgh

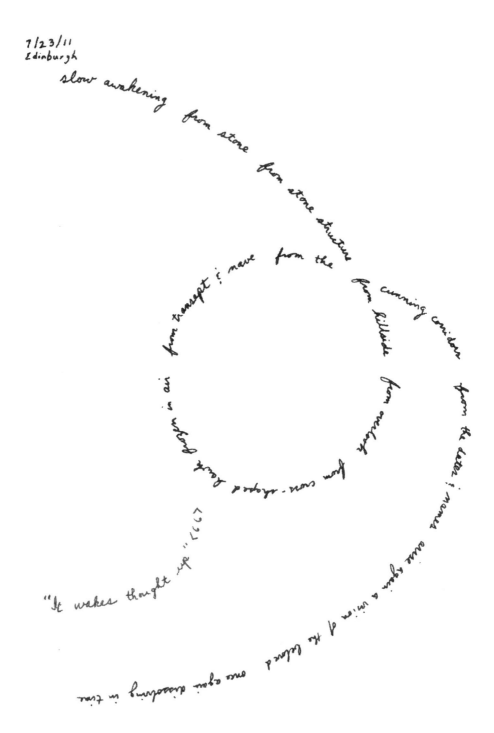

slow awakening from stone from stone structure from hillside from overlook from cross-shaped dark pages in air from transept & nave from the cunning corridors from the letters & names arise again a union of the beloved once again dissolving in time

"It wakes thought up" <69>

to find the loop in sound to go on to hear the next fiddler come into play a minor key as if the melody were in reverse

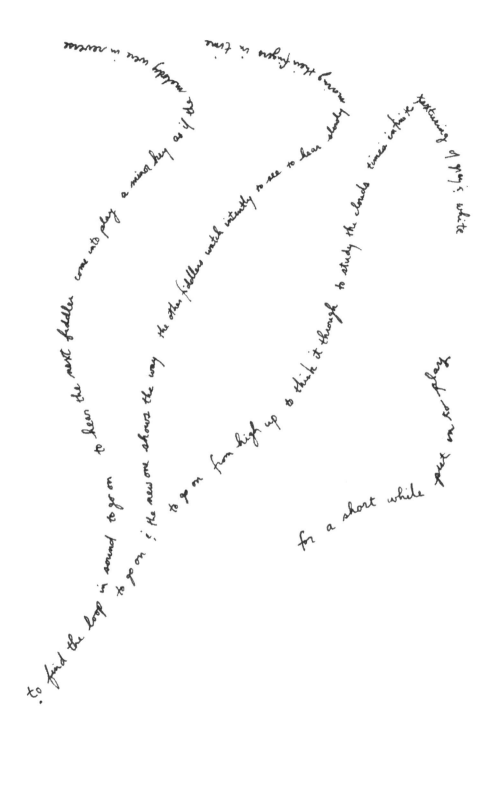

to go on ; the new one shows the way the other fiddlers watch intently to see to hear slowly moving their fingers in time

to go on from high up to think it through to study the clouds time's infinite texturing of gray's white

for a short while quiet on to play

7/30/11

i kiss the rock of IS   i sing the rock of ages   Little Sparta   gardens of perfection   paradise of the carved word   slowly engrave the way   a lifetime placed in making   a hidden force

widow   shadow   meadow

flow through time

a passerby

"One might give the name 'inspiration' to this intrigue of infinity in which I make myself   do you want something from me   arcs of sound take shape   as if i were awake

"it orders; [il ordonne]." <76>

the author of what I hear." <76>

7/31/11

as that portion of the pillar's length

all architectures

from which fell

once it was

brutal good which fact is

so said

as then all fall from

some

gives rise to these

time gives rise to pillar made of light

// errant path of light //

each

empty sky the name of men

of these

spoke to the wheel of light

fastened

habitable worlds hidden in words

by an

built it slowly over time

invisible

as that which emanates from

kind

8/2/11
8/3/11

it is with reference to a bowed beam a sounding board strings cat gut or synthetic stretched

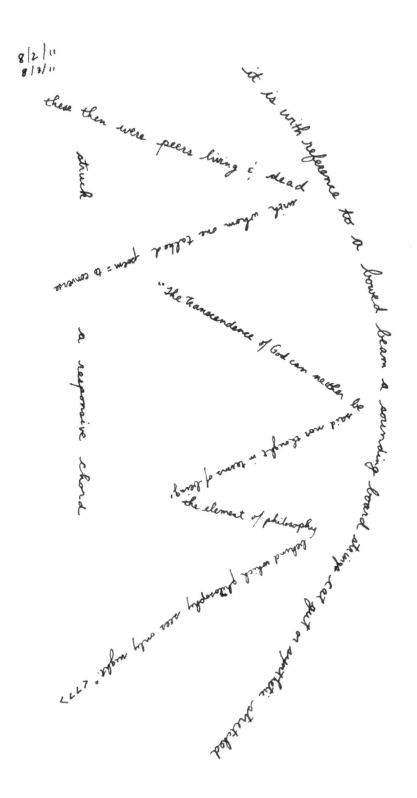

these then were peers living & dead

with whom one talked poem = to converse

"The transcendence of God can neither be

said nor thought in terms of being,

the element of philosophy

behind which philosophy sees only night." <77>

struck a responsive chord

8/17/11
LA

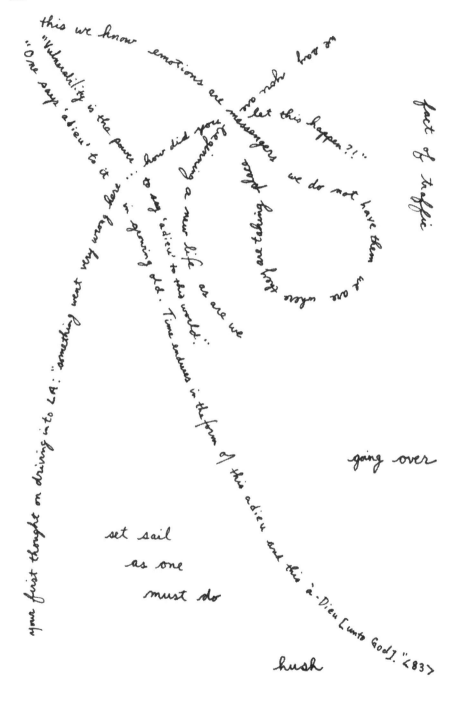

this we know emotions are messengers we do not have them we are where they are taking place

"Vulnerability is the power ... how did you let this happen?!"

we say you are beginning a new life as are we

"One says 'adieu' to it is growing old. Time endures in the form of this adieu and this à-Dieu [unto God]." <83>

to say 'adieu' to this world:

your first thought on driving into LA: "something went very wrong here ...

fact of traffic

going over

set sail
as one
must do

hush

8/18/11
LA

i ask

are there other instances of

we look forward to

paying homage is costly there is no other way just a few stories on top of everything else

"The new idea finds itself not on the basis of the prior, but by its sublimation." LG87

"though the passivity of aging (a withdrawal that, perhaps, exists not to mourn death itself" LG87

"I am clothed in a form; I am where my being hides me." LG87

8/20/11
LA

natural light

if emotions are messenger

to each is given -m- if a particular path of decay

word or if: "the impossibility of my declining the adventure." <92>

"as one cannot be replaced for death." <93>

"There is not a single thing in a great spirituality
that would be absent from another great spirituality." <93>

to waken
as then

it may not be

so momentous

after all

8/22/11
LA

“Im Shamo'a, Tishma'a”
“if you listen you will understand
much more”
<94>

“but a waiting
without an awaited” <95>

“one knows... that there is nothing to do: one will have to die one's death” <98>

“I think that God has no meaning outside the search for God” <95>

“On time as a
question” <95>

but because it is a human life

“asleep on Jacob's pillow stone”
asleep with head upon
the stone that
is

9/10/11

"Consciousness as reminiscence glorifies, in the representation,

from arriving light are we at the end of something a certain twilight that is through i knew it what was it nothing more than the vibrating

the ultimate sign of presence." <103>

tell the roof

"a duration of presence,

"Consciousness makes and renders presence

but tell it slant

or a duration as presence" <102>

it is the life of presence." <102>

light so bright suffering coming edge to edge with them beside you in your own blank immediacy chanting silently words coming to mind with their own pulsation

"This is a consciousness that has already been forgotten for the benefit of the present beings: it withdraws itself from appearance [l'apparaître] to give room to these beings," <103>

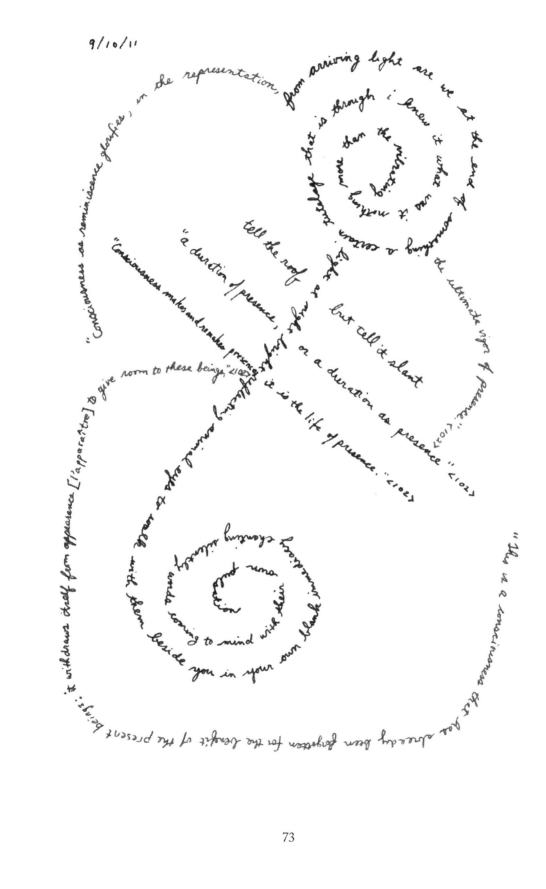

9/17/11

"All people are conscious of an attraction to certain aspects of the Torah and an incapacity to react to others." <AS/Rebbes/139>

who sleeps in: sleeps around who sleeps within:

who turns to or is turning into who or slowly knowing

"the ultimate affair of the soul" <104>

that makes time & our life in it

if it is motion rotation: revolution the changing light :-

"The soul, in the passive synthesis of aging and of its ad-vent, in its life, would be the original question, even the unto-God itself [l'à-Dieu même]." <108>

"Time as a question: an un-balanced relationship to the Infinite, to that which could not be comprehended: neither encompassed, nor touched,

a tearing of the correlation <108>

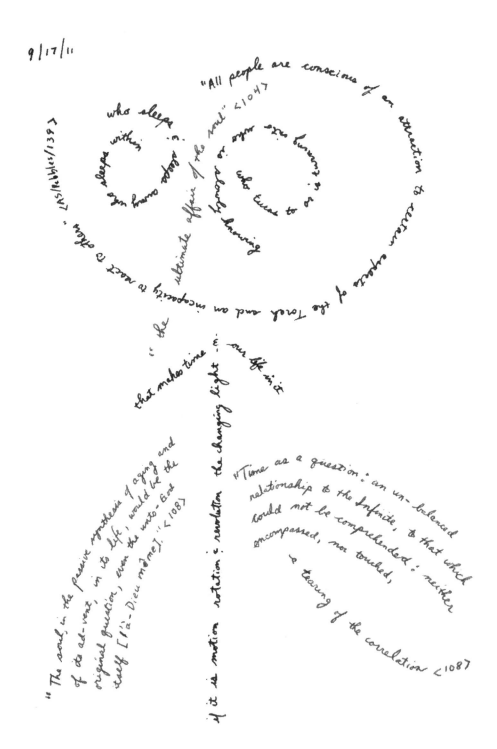

9/22/11
honolulu

who comes to mind that is this place that is this time that comes to mind turn as it may be a swell & take it home for another i know the making of the book is his given instrument "for to believe is precisely this dialectical wavering" Cross

for one i know the horn the given instrument of his singing each turn it is a yearning feel the returning instrumental in our singing what comes to mind take a turn feel the swell & take it home

at each turning turn & thinking here of thee i sing those on the horizon

feel the swell & take it home

9/23/11
honolulu

voices from the public address
echo & float away applause

"this question
about the meaning of meaning...

this kinship of meaning and knowledge...

"the 'gesture' of Being carried out by beings, inasmuch as they assert themselves as beings,...

Of it is an adventure of the intelligible...

to become aware
of the question itself,
which calls to it" <111>

it supposes this substance, beneath all motion...
a reign of a fundamental rest in the verb 'to be,'
which the grammarians lightly call auxiliary...

That this rest reigns
precisely beneath the vault
of fixed stars,... Through this rest,
where everything has a place and is
identified, everything takes place." <112>

as happening at the edge wading out into swimming into & beside an unimaginable depth an adventuring barely at the edge of
exercise or recreation you are moving into these swells arising at the edge of call it the sea shoreline of a governing emptiness

9/24/11
honolulu

are we not being shown something else is losing the way whose way was it are there not those

he says you do not realize the pain of love

sits with his parents he has a sweet full smile it is a little off he finds something to talk about something he knows it is fishing is the others as pictures on his cell phone

the older boy at the table he is a man he is thirty

or finitude — or is a comprehension of being " (1143)

old pound could not make it alone perhaps it does not ; only a difference of degree

a difference of degree he says he ; was

"the Being" in the world — even the death, which reconciles

so lost in a simple place can't find my way back he names it cognitive loss

can't follow the conversation

9/26/11
honolulu

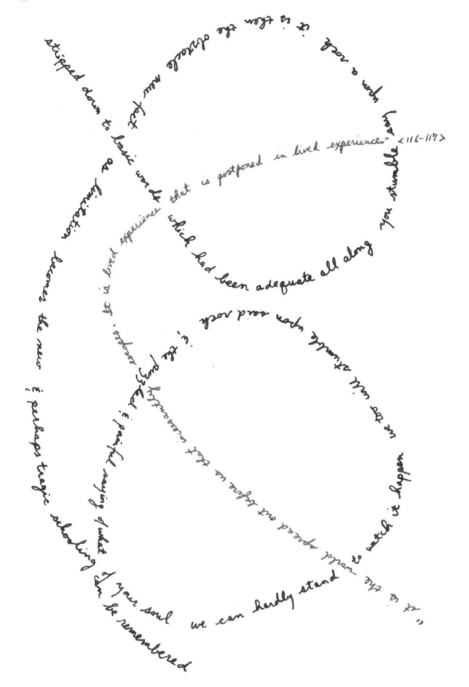

stripped down to basic words
which had been adequate all along
you stumble upon a rock
it is then the obstacle new fact
as limitation becomes the new & perhaps tragic schooling can be remembered

we too will stumble upon said rock
& the puzzled & painful saying of what of your soul
we can hardly stand & watch it happen

"it is the world spread out before us that incessantly escapes. It is lived experience that is postponed in lived experience" <116–117>

9/28/11
honolulu

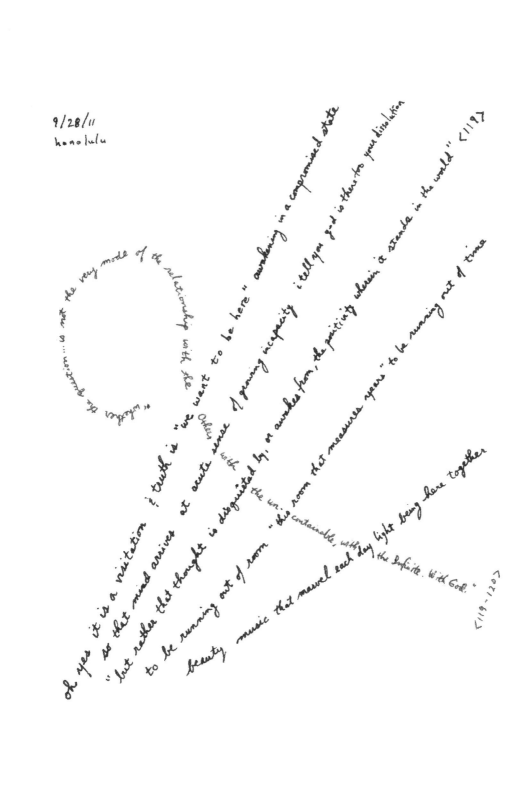

oh yes it is a visitation i truth is "we want to be here" awakening in a compromised state

so that mind arrives at acute sense of growing incapacity i tell you god is there too your dissolution

" but rather that thought is disquieted by, or awakes from, the positivity wherein it stands in the world" <119>

to be running out of room "this room that measures years" to be running out of time

beauty music that marvel each day light being here together

"whether the question ... is not the very mode of the relationship with the Other with the un-containable, with the Infinite. With God." <119-120>

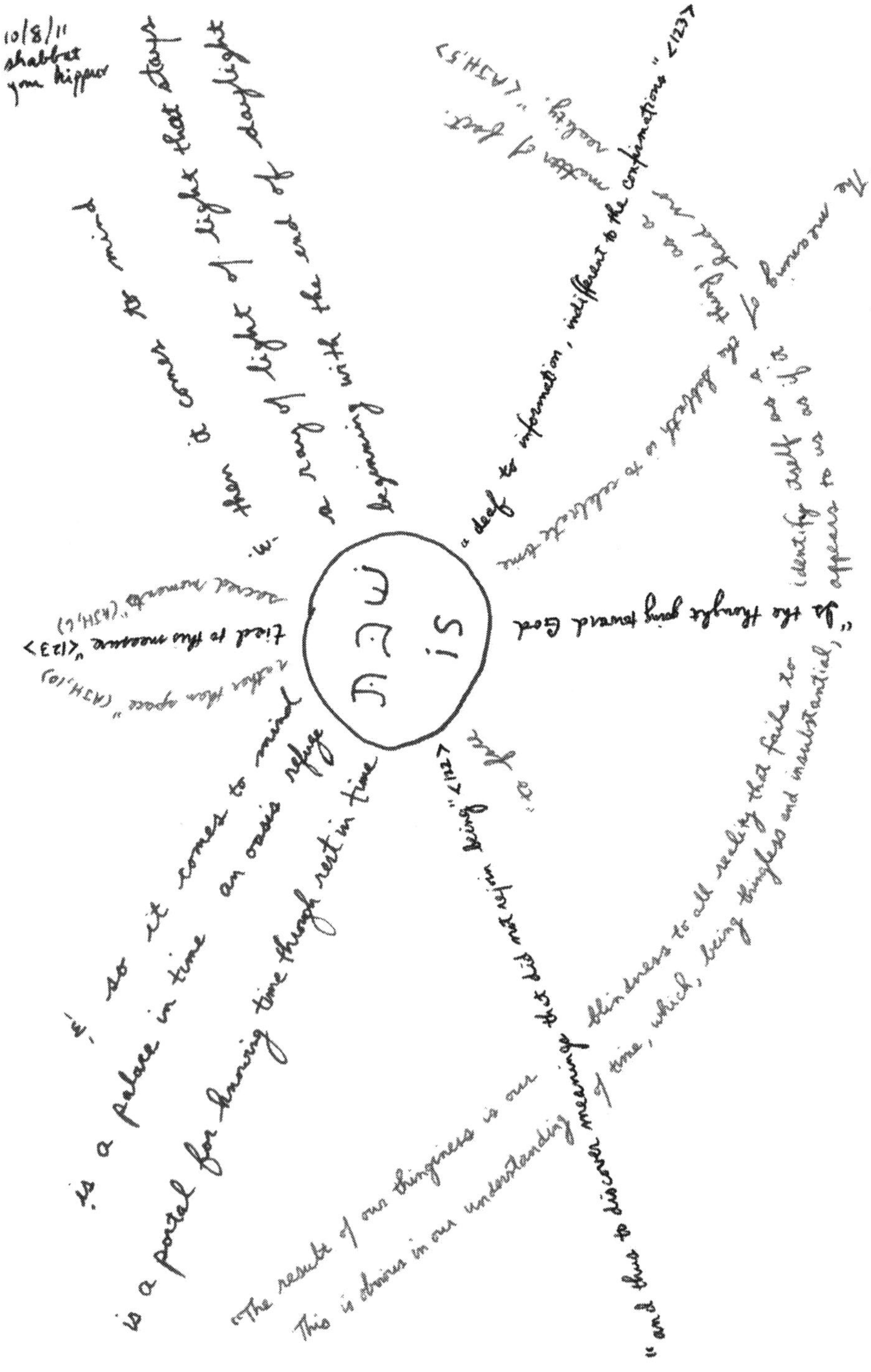
10/8/11
shabbat
yom kippur
שבת
is
then it comes to mind
a ray of light of light that stays
beginning with the end of daylight
a deaf to information, indifferent to the confirmations" <123>
to the thought going toward God"
tied to the measure" <123>
is a palace in time
so it comes to mind
is a portal for knowing time through rest in time
an oasis refuge
"and thus to discover meaning that did not rely on being" <123>
"The result of our thingness is our
This is obvious in our understanding
blindness to all reality that fails to
of time, which, being thingless and insubstantial,
identify itself as
appears to us

10/22/11

"What pioneers reappear in the established order. Our modernity would not depend solely
upon the certitudes of History and Nature, but upon an alternation: Recovery
and Rupture ... This is an alternation where the moment of recovery
is not more true than that of rupture; wherein lastly there
is no more sense than the face-to-face with the neighbor.

take your time

take your
sweet time

it takes time

in its own time

there's no time like the present

is it time it is time

what time is it

it is high time you got going

whenever you take a notion

"... would define time itself; time in its
enigmatic diachrony: a tendency without an
outcome, an intending without coincidence." <134>

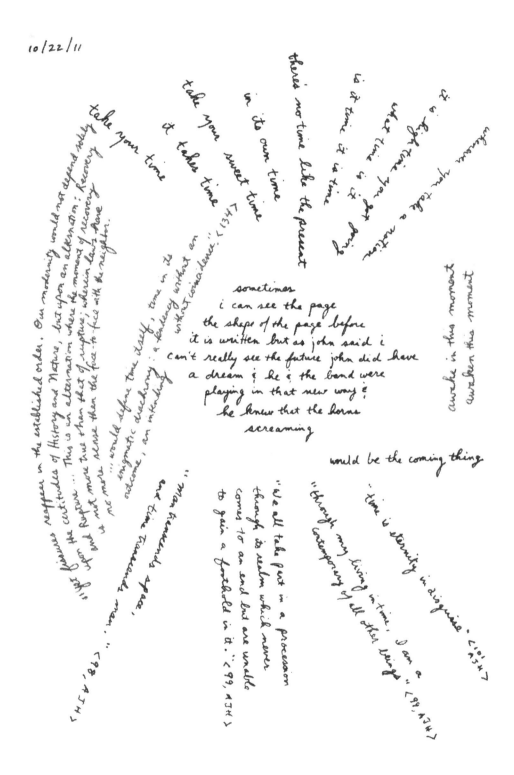

sometimes
i can see the page
the shape of the page before
it is written but as john said i
can't really see the future john did have
a dream & he & the band were
playing in that new way &
he knew that the horns
screaming

would be the coming thing

awake in this moment
awaken this moment

"Man transcends space,
and time transcends man." <98, AJH>

"We all take part in a procession
through its realm which never
comes to an end but are unable
to gain a foothold in it." <99, AJH>

"Through my living in time, I am a
contemporary of all other beings" <99, AJH>

"time is eternity in disguise." <101, AJH>

"... and that knowledge of the world is a satisfaction; as though this knowledge filled a need." <139>

being time

wan
One life
won

"Does not all that occurs in the human psyche, and all that takes place there, end up by being known?" <137>

10/29/11

"Such is spirit, ... where the process of knowing is 'the movement of being itself'" <140>

10/30/11
10/31/11

So it is slowly furrowing thinking in its own sweet time taking a turn a page of changing shape as it takes shape in this instance of thinking sing then what light is who finds the time is right who writes or needs the needed words & in that moment catches fire on the turnstile clicks & you enter nearly a lifetime of words wandering & searching a low morning a distant rumbling a barely audible hum a night silence having entered the turning of the words hear you are hand eyes mind engaged spirit restored to turn again & so move on

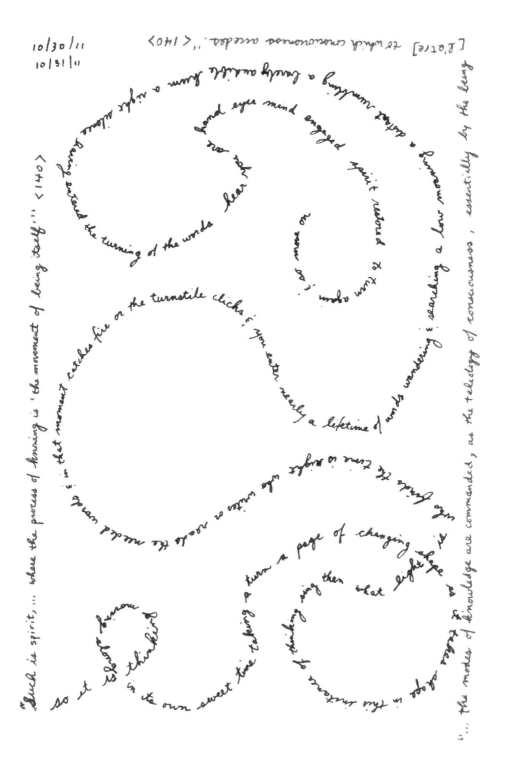

"... the modes of knowledge are commanded, as the teleology of consciousness, essentially by the being [L'être] to which consciousness accedes." <140>

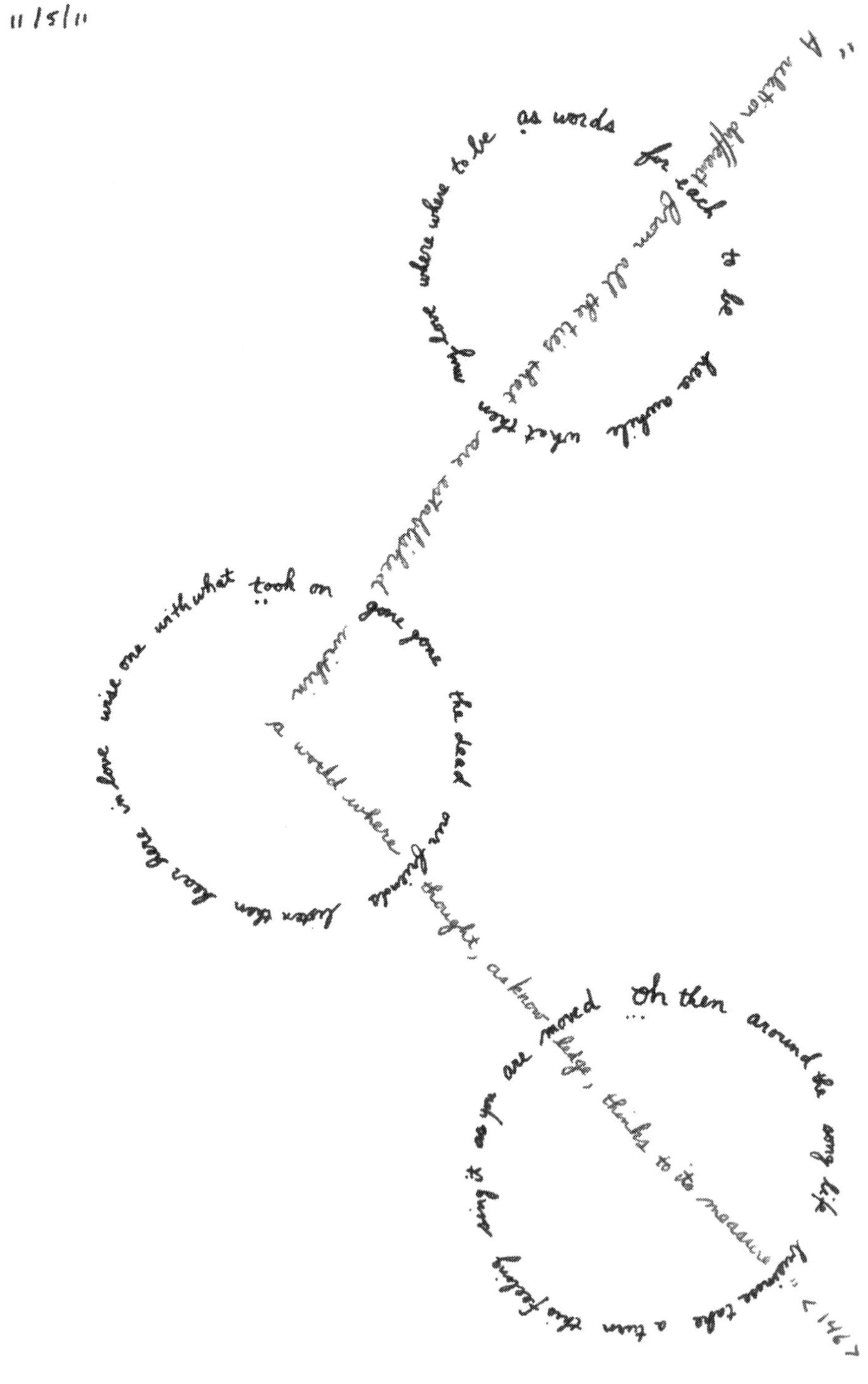
11/5/11
" A relation different from all the ties that are established within a world where thought, as knowledge, thinks to its measure " < 146 >
for each to be here awhile what then my love where where to be as words
gone gone the dead our friends listen then here here in love wise one with what took on
Oh then around the song life business take a turn the feeling sing it as you are moved

11/6/11

a lifetime not enough time to know what we might be

"as in the psyche as experience" (1948)

and so we move along a the we being human beings

in time an instance is a looking its one

a loop in time to ask upon questions of being

each a loop a loop of many such inquiries this thinking to light

so much depends upon the weight of what you have borrowed through time your momentary loan to being moved to say to call it what it is bringing to light this dark time

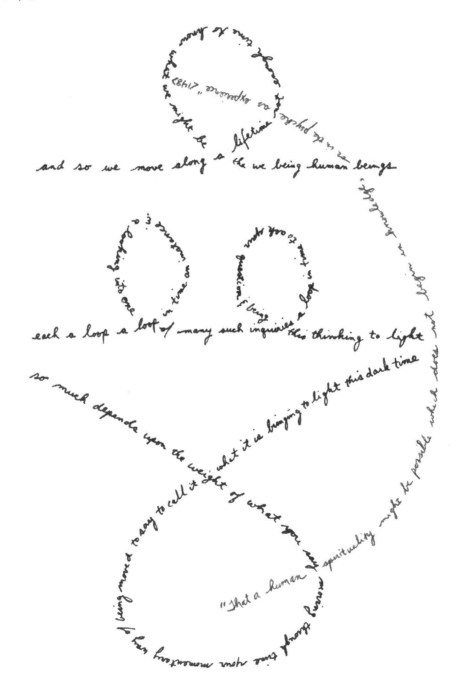

"That a human spirituality might be possible which does not begin in humility,"

11/20/11

the horizon of your personal journey

keep your eye on

. it comes to mind through the hand writing the ship no longer possible as we are victims of our own productive stupidity and our own undoing the ship is going down we must not say so please sing everything else that comes to mind

"Does thought have meaning only through the knowledge of the world?... Or does the meaning in a meaningful thought exist, perhaps, in a way that is older than presence or re-presentable presence; that is, in a way more present and better than these?" <151>

11/27/11

“... produced in a thought understood as a thought of ... The very breath of spirit in thought

would be ... knowledge. ... The cognitive intention is thus a free act. The soul is affected but

... without passivity. It regains possession of itself in taking the given upon itself according to its intention.

... seeking you wanted to go home i seek

great stillness slow cold front moving through & i'll be seeing you in the same light, also loss of elasticity:

... the grace of thinking what could i say to you that would matter or that would change anything

everything ends by being known, we do not think that knowledge would be the meaning and the end of everything.” <145>

The soul awakes. ... Everything is contained in the opening of the soul: presence

“Even if is candor itself.” <154-155>

so dark so soon where ted has gone before the darkest part of year so dark so soon the light arrives by faith
in turning round this small space where i am quiet eye who speaks a sudden song & makes the singing great
archway over the dark day
arriving into light

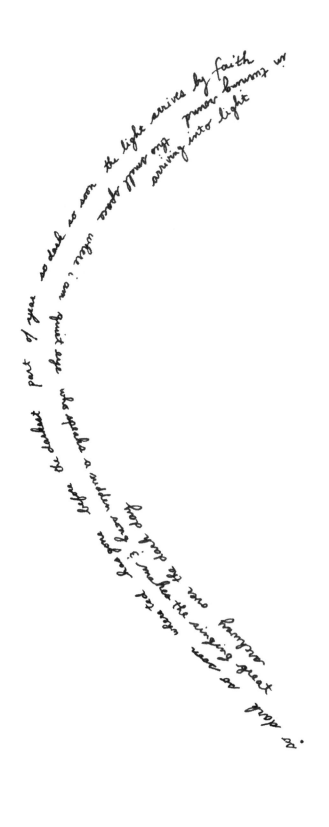

for theodore enslin

d. 11/22/11

12/16/11

i listen to what the angel sings yes the angel sings

i am not the angel singing

i'm with my eyes; right hand this is singing

"I have given you to write"

angel sings.

i am not the angel singing

Fine, I said. Firmament.

"I call bullshit on firmament. There's no such thing as firmament."

There is, though, I said. It's in Torah.

"What's it mean, then?"

I said, No one really knows what it means. In Hebrew, it's the place where Adonai resides, but it's a bad translation. It's really more like border—it's confusing.

"I don't think that's fair," she said. "If you don't know what it means, you can't use it."

That's your rule, I said. I said, That's not my rule.

<The Instructions, 104>

12/17/11

and so to say bright luminous warm light cold vision

breath of the sacred her i) to what the hidden H to what calls in miracle of infinite combinations of how many letters words human bodies as infinite as variable as human being turn the word wheel of the cell how that plays registers of breath articulating change for what in sound human here am i

full through here i am a few a day on opening &

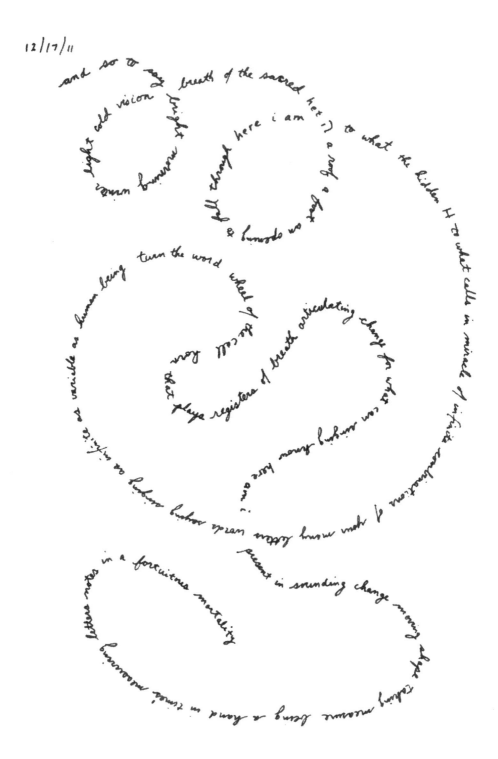

present in sounding change moving shape taking measure being a hand in time moving letters notes in a fortuitous mortality

12/21/11

"disrupting the equilibrium of the darkness turning say a leaning into greater light

mystery of what we are here as: enigma a.

"It commends a thinking that is older and more awakened than knowledge or experience" <1960>

of the day that turns shortest day the way of least light equal and impassive and of knowing" <1961>

sing then the

sing then all we do is: who we do it for

"Whereas the thought awakened to the face, or by the face ... a thought that not a thought of ... but from the outset a thought for ... of" <1960–1961>

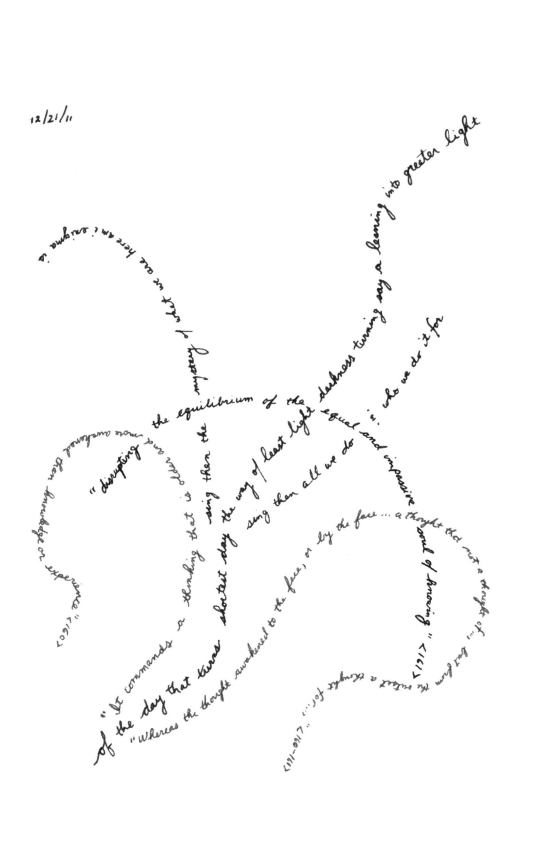

12/22/11

his books include

learning into a

over

tending toward

arching

it all depends

"speculation... has a presentiment of deathe mystery" <163>

her writing

reached the point

"of an inimitable, unfathomable God," <163>

zero aside our writing never arrives

we are able to feel

such currency

place of daily light

"that no relationship could be affirmed, because He is a term in no relation" <166>

this the human neighborhood

12/24/11

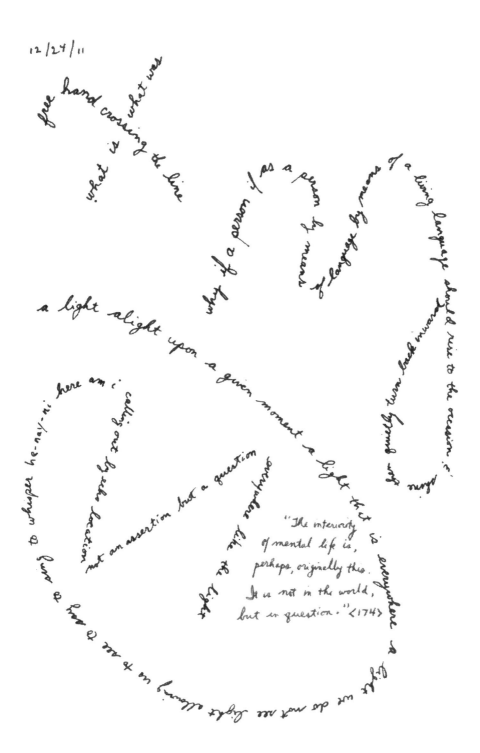

free hand crossing the line

what is what was

why if a person / as a person by means of language by means of a living language should rise to the occasion i: when i do quietly turn back inward

a light alight upon a given moment a light that is everywhere a light we do not see light allowing us to see to hear a song to whisper he-nay-ni here am i:

calling out by site location

not an assertion but a question

everywhere like the light

"The interiority of mental life is, perhaps, originally this. It is not in the world, but in question." <174>

12/25/11

you might ask

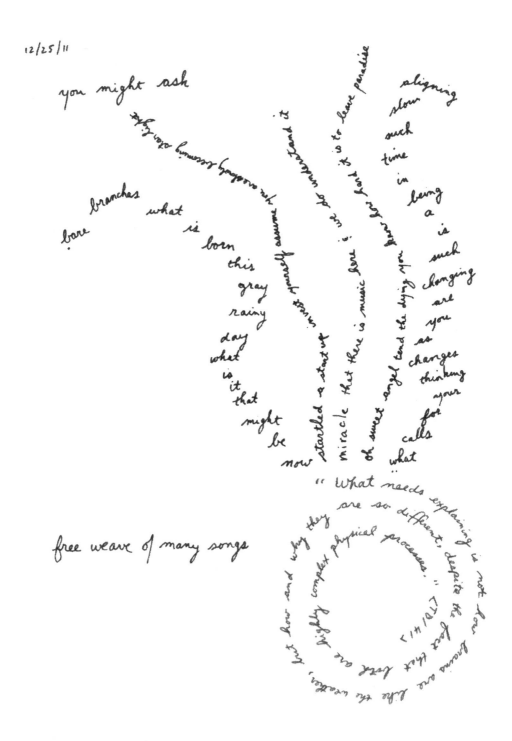

bare branches what is born this gray rainy day what is it that might be now

startled a start up invest yourself assume you are slowly becoming starlight

miracle that there is music here ∴ we do understand it

oh sweet angel tend the dying you know how hard it is to leave paradise

what calls for your thinking changes as you are changing such is a being in time such slow aligning

free weave of many songs

" What needs explaining is not how brains are like the weather, but how and why they are so different, despite the fact that both are highly complex physical processes. " (TD/413)

12/29/11

to return then to the invisible fact of being

"to take up once again the problem of ontology, which is implicitly resolved by each one of us, even if by forgetting it." <1>

take your sweet time

small recall certain but invisible end

"or, if you like, it is because being is intelligible, that there is humanity" <2>

that you suffer

12/30/11

To be complete, just to be engaged, to merged with what we think, launched — the dramatic event of being-in-the-world." <3>

"To think is no longer to understand it as a whole" <3>

into wisdom to enfold it, we are very busy invisible mysteries become hidden in plain sight before our very eyes miracles

out of circuit of intelligence

"We exist with the real" <4>

in a

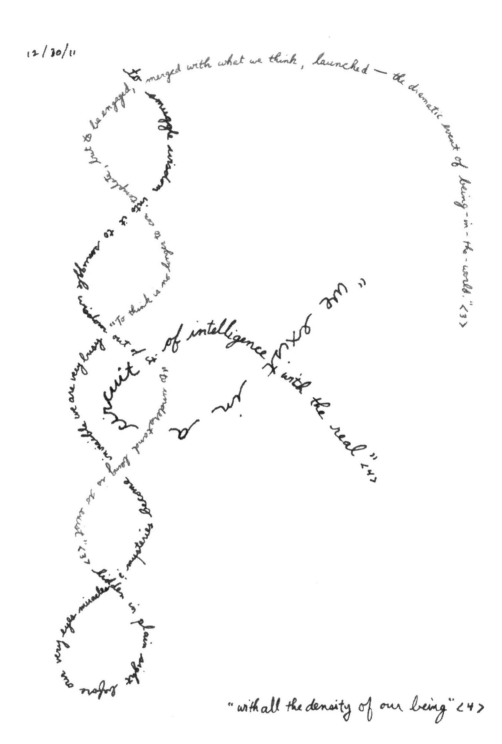

"with all the density of our being" <4>

1/8/12

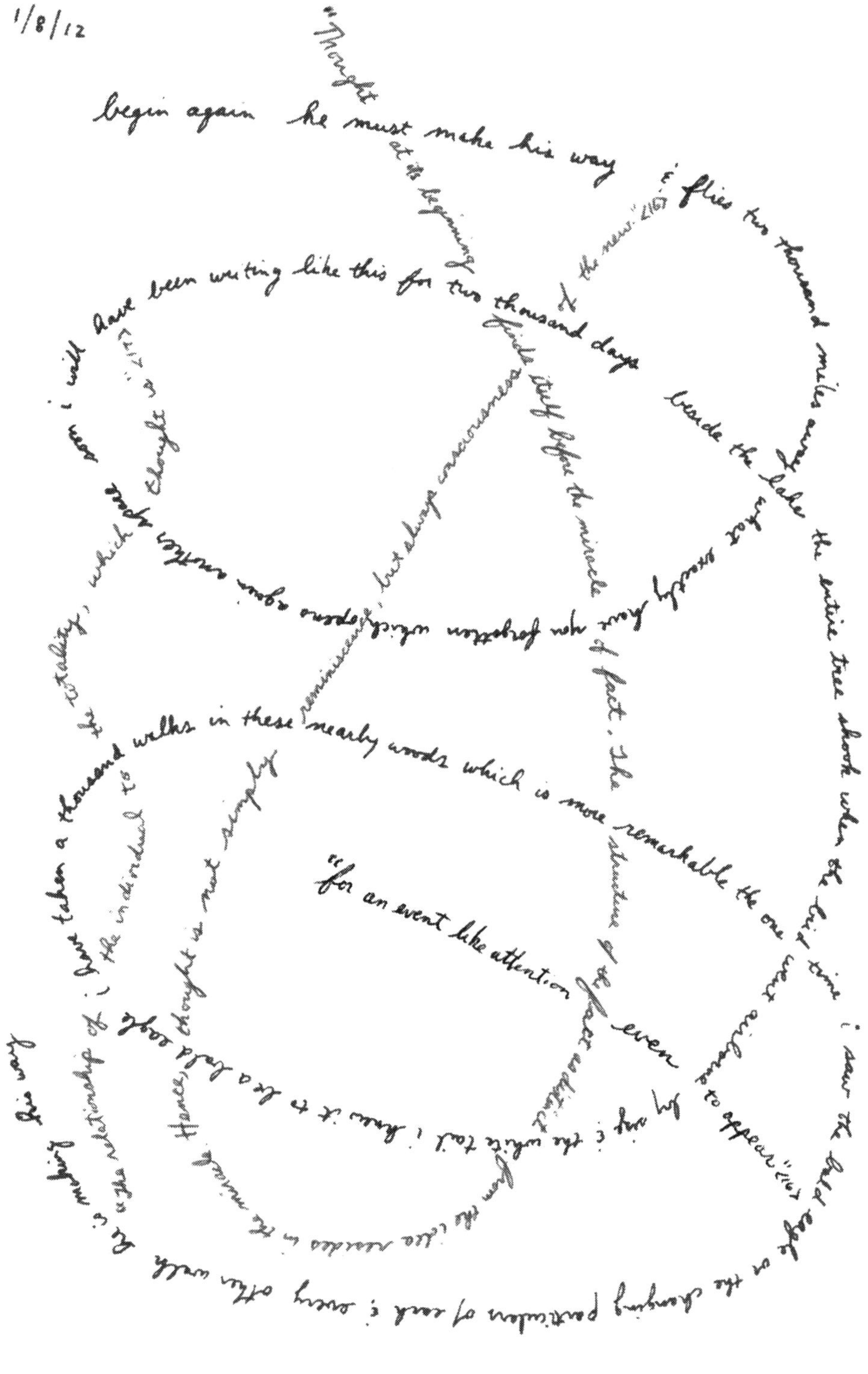
begin again he must make his way
"Thought at its beginning
flies two thousand miles
i will have been writing like this for two thousand days
beside the lake the entire tree shook
finds itself before the miracle of fact, the structure of
but always consciousness
i have taken a thousand walks in these nearby woods which is more remarkable the one
"for an event like attention
thought is not simply
the individual to
even
to appear."

1/14/12

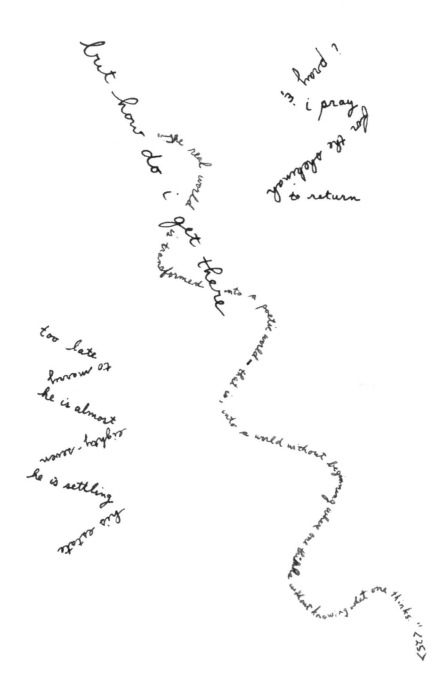

but how do i get there

the real world is transformed into a poetic world — that is, into a world without boundaries where one thinks without knowing what one thinks." <225>

is hard?
i pray
for the afterworld
to return

too late
to morrow
he is almost
eighty-seven
he is settling
his estate

1/15/12

only poems talk to poems what i remember now do you each in his particular ribbon of time being here thinking about it passing the time the daily changing light until it isn't

"The work presents its author in the absence of the author." <29>

"No one is identical to himself. Beings have no identity. Faces are masks. Behind the faces that speak to us and to whom we speak, we look for the clockwork and microscopic springs of souls. As sociologists, we seek social laws which behave ... Like storyteller influences, governing the others wishes and smiles; as philologists and historians, we will even deny that anyone can be the author of his discourse." <24>

All thought is poetic, pure doing, without any connection with principle, without any beginning" <31>

Transcendence is what turns its face towards me." <34>

1/16/12

how did we used to think
how did we used to think about it
a glimpse
what am i forgetting
what exactly am i forgetting

if you say so
i'll consider it
"if only as a faithful reading of the facts" <39>
thats' the way i see it
at first i used to hear it

heenayni הִנֵּנִי heenayni chant it
here am i   now
not later
now   here am i
given over to the one who calls

1/21/12

because the poem contains everything because the poem is incomplete because each page says it all because each page requires another
& another because the poem is where i declare i am here because the poem goes on without me because the poem takes
its own course because the poem is yours because the poem belongs to no one because the poem is writing

why does the poem hold it all why does the poem leave out so much why does each page pray so fondly why does each page turn to the next
& the next why am i here in the poem why is the poem not ours why does the poem go on without us why does the poem make its own
way why is the poem mine why is the poem a changing place of possession why is the poem where writing comes to write it

"duration does not delineate a formal dimension in which being flows
but is at the same time being and experience of being" (427)

"The pregnancy of feeling is no longer interpreted as a reverberation
of a knowing about an affectivity enclosed in itself, but as [illegible]
with being, more direct than sensation" (427)

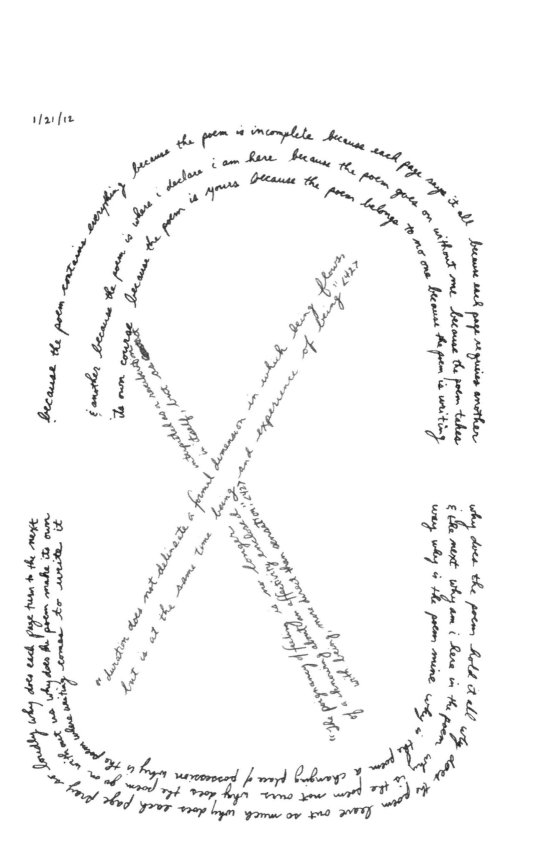

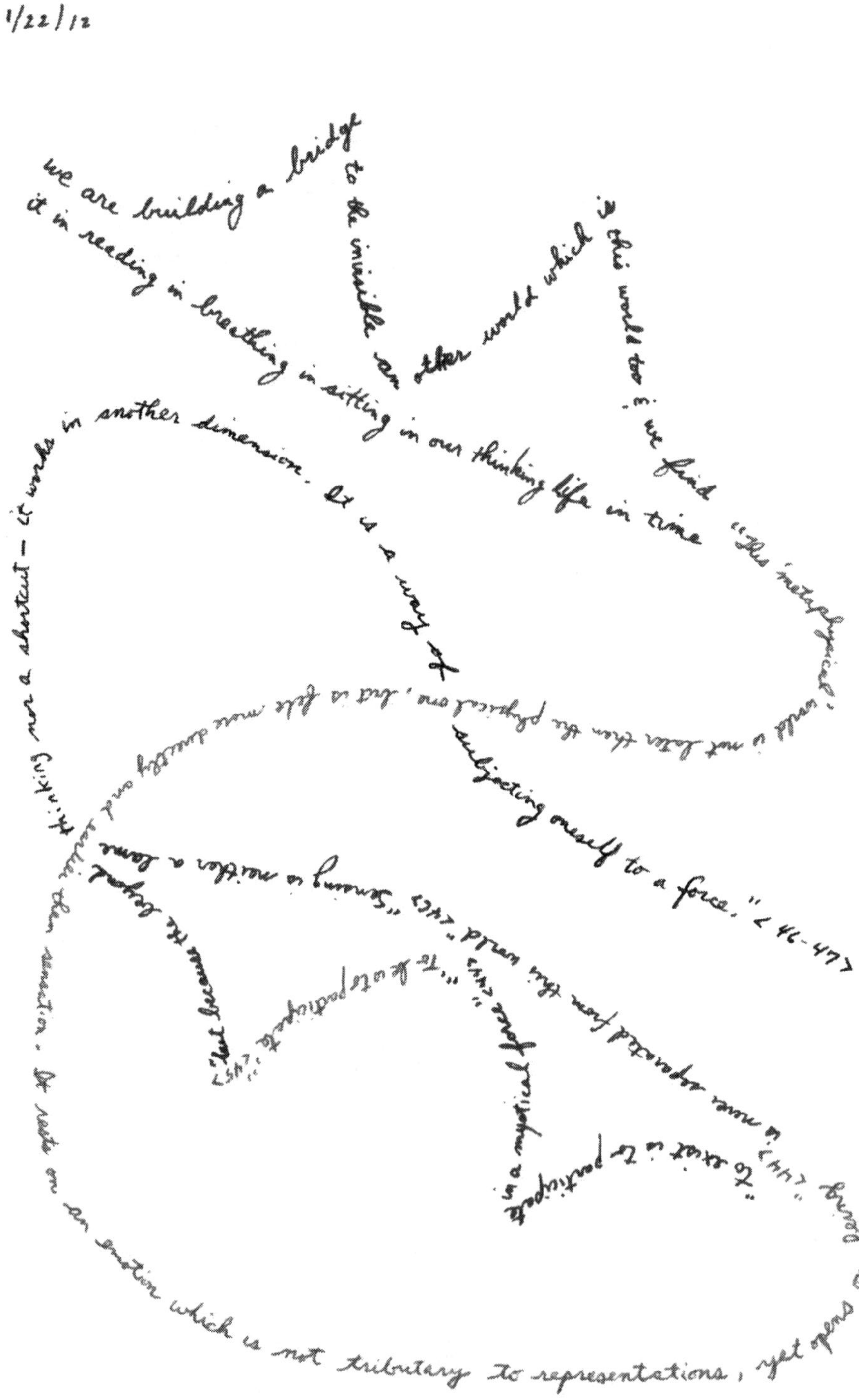
1/22/12
we are building a bridge to the invisible an other world which is this world too; we find
it in reading in breathing in sitting in our thinking life in time
"The 'metaphysical' world is not better than the physical one, but is felt more directly and earlier than sensation. It rests on an emotion which is not tributary to representations, yet opens a beyond." <44>
"To exist is to participate in a mystical force" <44>
"To fail to participate" <45>
is more separated from this world." <44> "Samsara is neither a same
"but because the beyond
thinking not a shortcut — it works in another dimension. It is a way to subjecting oneself to a force." <46-47>

1/28/12

light again in words
with nothing but life
is making a way toward who knows what
" from being itself that fills the instant " <48>

so today; breath as guide light life to say
next when you of the next time take: up this twisting

its homeland in the world of ideas" <49>
" that illumination that reveals to the soul

this given instant is the
to write to shape these words

2/4/12

I have given you to write.

"It is up to you how much of the immeasurable becomes reality for you." <B/83>

"Spirit is word." <B/89>

Listen to the voice & write exactly what it says

"The relation with the Infinite is not a knowledge, but a proximity, preserving the excessiveness of the uncontainable which grazes the surface." <58> "So there is an end; but a new wisdom, a new rationality begins, a new notion of spirit." <62>

2/7/12
Havana

"Consciousness which already
allows itself to be forgotten
for the benefit of present entities,
it withdraws itself from appearing
to make room for them." <49>

somos
juntos
united in our differences

pensar es sentir
sí
sentir es pensar

sentir es pensar
sí
pensar es sentir

your rhythm your way of saying it
which we find fallen into our midst without our knowing whence or how, and already circulating" <70>

dentro
de las palabras

melody of

recurring
phrase

"We have recourse to the notion
of a horizontal religion,
remaining on the earth
of human beings" <70>

"The idea of God and even the origins of the word God –

listening post

"Why is there saying?" <71>

"It is a spirituality granted to the founding firmness of the earth" <69>

2/9/12
Havana

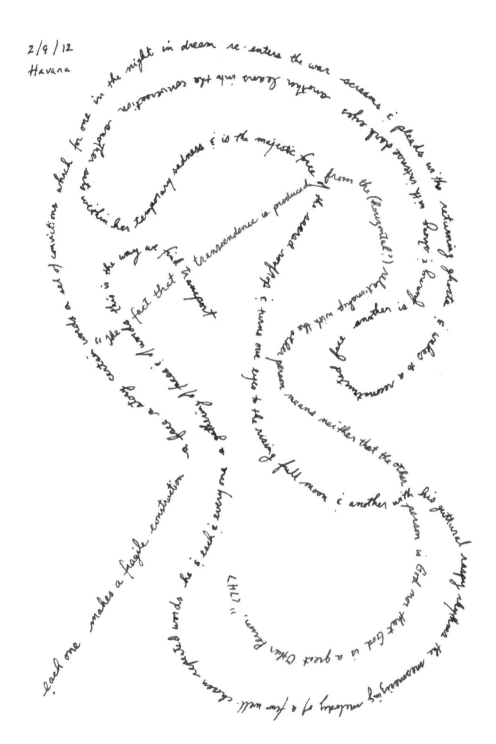

Each one makes a fragile construction a house or a story creates words a set of convictions which for one in the night in dream re-enters the war screams & pleads with the returning ghosts & wakes to a reconstructed face another is fuming & sings with unfinished dark echo another floats into the conversation within her temporary sadness & is the majestic face from the (hospital?) relationship with the other person means neither that the other person is God nor that God is a great Other Person." (EHL)

& this is the way we find transport & transcendence is produced the second power & deeper & turns one eyes to the rising full moon & another with his guttural happy rhythms the mesmerizing melody of a few well-chosen repeated words he & each & every one a gathering of faces & words & the fact that

2/10/12

the poem is the cry is the song is the cry is the song is the cry is the poem of the individual held in the power of the State

path of light

"faith is precisely that infinite preoccupation with the self that keeps you alert to risk everything, that internal preoccupation for knowing whether you really have faith" 274-75

i have given you to right

we will carry on

somos juntos

in your country or in mine the smiling face of the evil bureaucrat she will always have that she does it in friendship in honesty & for our own good

2/19/12

at any moment the state

at any moment the state may intervene

they will try to stop us

they will have their reasons

they do not show an individual face

the state delivers its message through someone else

at any moment the state

for the moment we are occupying this page we make no demands somos

"the justification of the neighbor's pain is certainly the source of all immorality" <99>

cannot break us apart somos

juntos

juntos somos

"A state in which the interpersonal relationship is impossible, in which it is directed in advance by the determinism proper to the state, is a totalitarian state" <105>

"It is perhaps there that the for-the-other, the most upright relation to the other—is the most profound adventure of subjectivity, its ultimate intimacy." <99>

intermittent early morning rain

return to the body in being

stop & listen

"the arrangement of some piece of being's delicate clockwork." [78]

"But taken as ontic knowledge, and compared
to the coherent, communicable and
universal results of scientific knowledge,
philosophy today has lost
all credence." [78]

do not

2/25/12

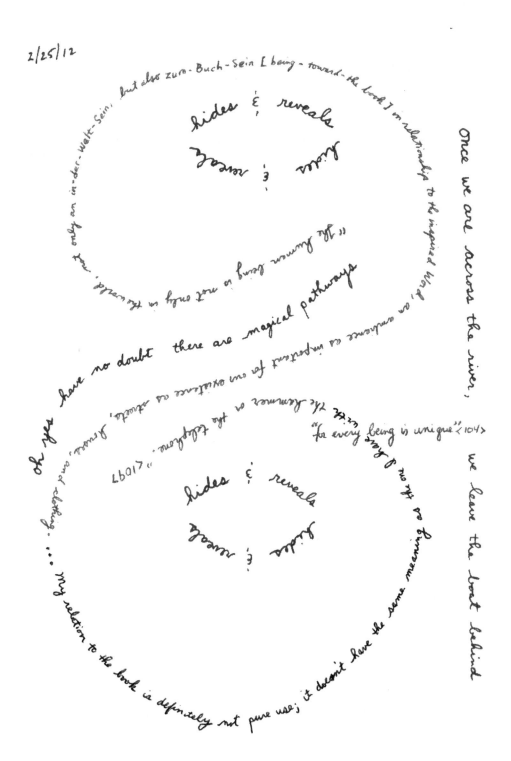

Once we are across the river, we leave the boat behind

"The human being is not only in the world, not only an in-der-Welt-Sein, but also zum-Buch-Sein [being-toward-the book] in relationship to the inspired Word, an ambience as important for our existence as streets, houses, and clothing. ... My relation to the book is definitely not pure use; it doesn't have the same meaning as the one I have with the hammer or the telephone." <107>

"For every being is unique" <104>

hides & reveals

reveals & hides

Oh yes have no doubt there are magical pathways

hides & reveals

reveals & hides

2/26/12

could this be a fork in the road time for you to make a decision what is the hold up what do you uphold

"the stranger in the earth," ... the stateless or homeless person, who does not enter. The interiority of the mental is perhaps originally this. Not in the world, but in question." [129]

"What thought knows is what it learns in its exposure to the other and thought's self." [125]

"... which goes blurred when thought [la pensée] is absorbed in what it thinks [le pensé]." [125]

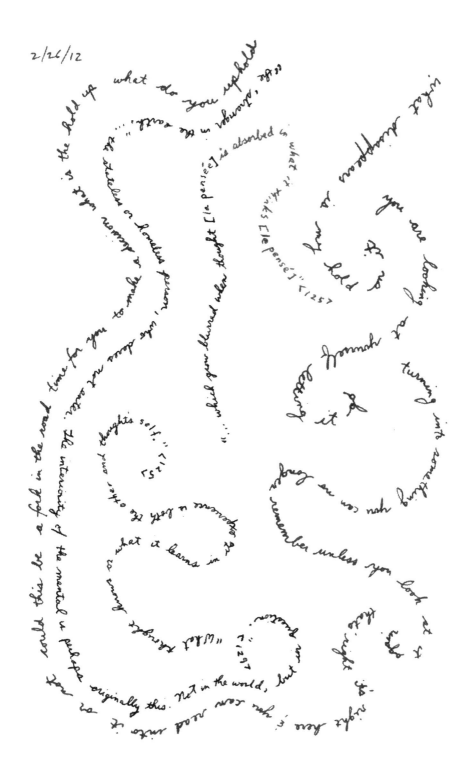

what disappears is how you hold on to it you are looking at yourself letting it go turning it into something you can no longer remember unless you look at it up. that's right it's right here is where you can read into it as how

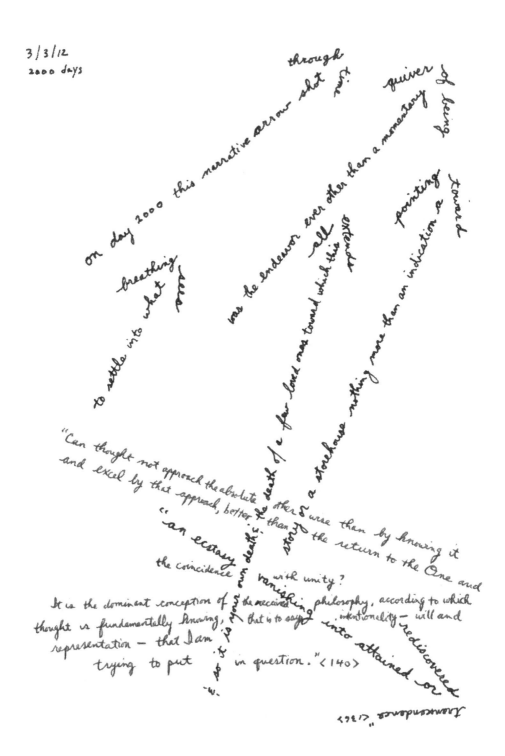

3/3/12
2000 days

on day 2000 this narrative arrow shot through time

to settle into what breathing sees

was the endeavor ever other than a momentary quiver of being

the death of a few loved ones toward which this all extends

story of a storehouse nothing more than an indication a pointing toward

"Can thought not approach the absolute otherwise than by knowing it and excel by that approach, better than the return to the One and the coincidence with unity? It is the dominant conception of the received philosophy, according to which thought is fundamentally knowing, that is to say intentionality — will and representation — that I am trying to put in question." <140>

"an ecstasy vanishing into attained or rediscovered transcendence" <126>

-ib. "so it is your own death:

3/4/12

opening & closing
front at once
what is happening
which
is
or a winding up
an unwinding
as an
here we
said to be
put into question

invisible frontier turned back by this insistent calling into question a finger pointing at the room "piece" what are you looking at each from one to the other a circuit in being one says history another says time slowly i am on the side of time which makes me ask oh then with our time here in this time can either of us say what did we do

duration of time" <1945>

as if it were some childhood of the mind to be outgrown" <1945>

"appears to an invisible death and mysterious foreboding" <1945>

a consolation for the failure of humility & equal being" <1948>

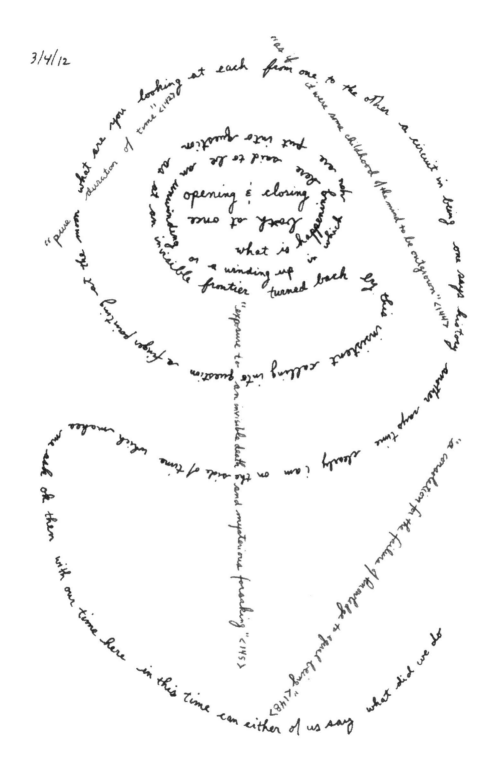

3/10/12

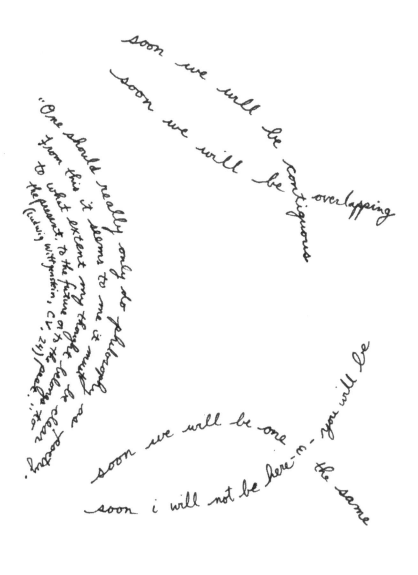

soon we will be contiguous

soon we will be overlapping

"One should really only do philosophy as poetry. From this it seems to me it must be clear to what extent my thought belongs to the present, to the future or to the past." (Ludwig Wittgenstein, C.V., 24)

soon we will be one — you will be

soon i will not be here — in — the same

are you here

3/11/12

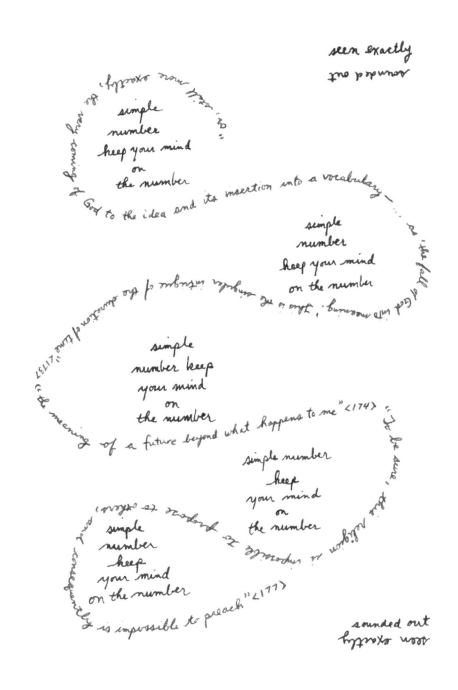

seen exactly
sounded out

"is still more exactly, the very coming of God to the idea and its insertion into a vocabulary— ... as the fall of God into meaning; this is the simplest intrigue of the duration of time" <173>

simple
number
keep your mind
on
the number

simple
number
keep your mind
on the number

"the meaning of a future beyond what happens to me" <174>

simple
number keep
your mind
on
the number

"To be sure, this religion is unspeakable as prayer, exactly, and consequently is impossible to preach" <177>

simple number
keep
your mind
on
the number

simple
number
keep
your mind
on the number

sounded out
seen exactly

3/17/12

"The call to holiness preceding the concern for existing." <216>

day or
night the heavens
like a field

"A spirituality that signifies equality between persons at peace." <190>

"With his notion of duration, he freed time from its obedience to astronomy." <198>

"creates silence, maintains silence, and protects it." <207>

"thought as the gathering and articulation of the event of being" <211-212>

having crossed over
we leave the rowboat
& walk on

"the original juncture of circumstances in which the infinite comes to the mind in its ambiguity of truth and freedom" <219>

i have served the book
a scribe
in being & time

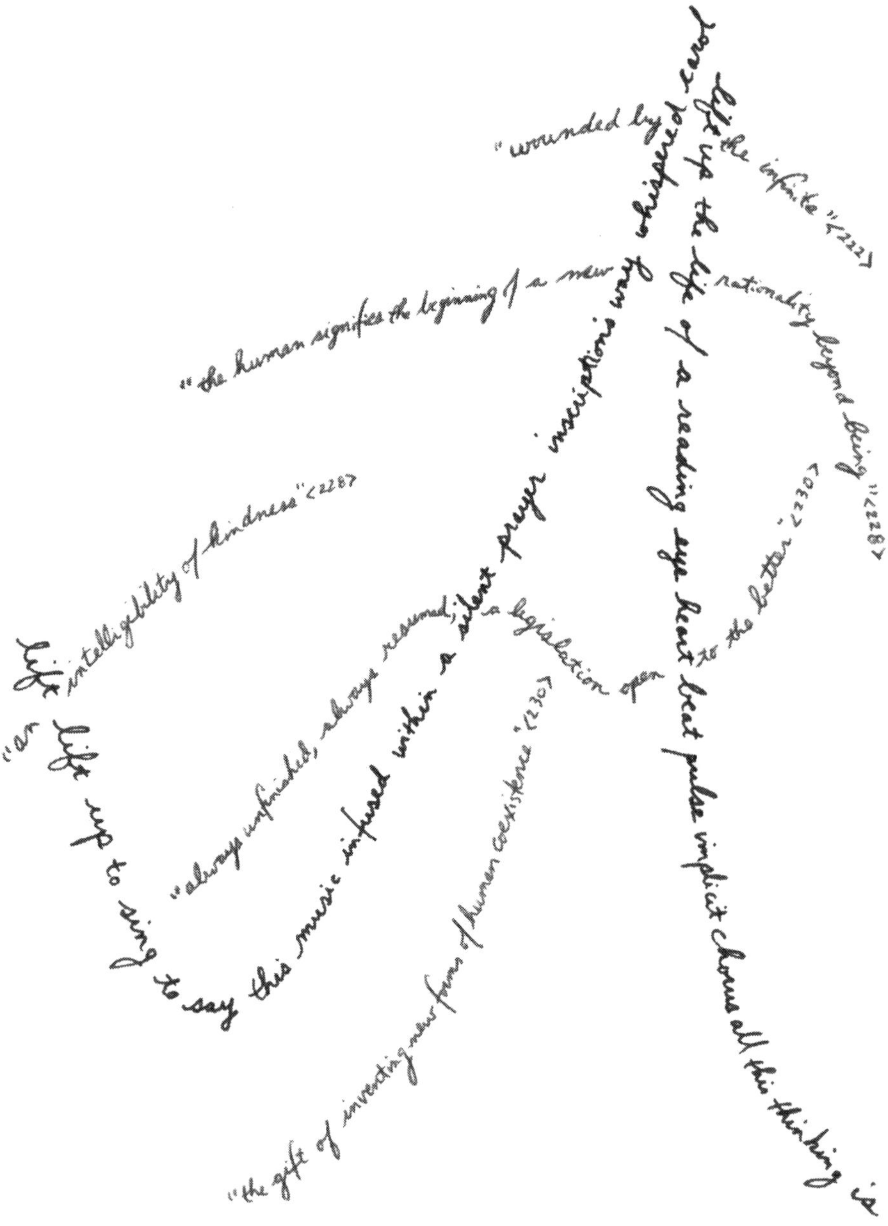
lift up the life of a reading eye heart beat pulse implicit chorus all this thinking is
"wounded by the infinite"<222>
rationality beyond being"<228>
to the better"<230>
a legislation open
sand whispered way inscriptions prayer silent a within infused music this say to sing to up lift
"the human signifies the beginning of a new
intelligibility of kindness"<228>
"always unfinished, always resumed;
"the gift of inventing new forms of human coexistence"<230>
lift
"as
lift up to sing to say this music infused within a silent prayer inscriptions way whispered sand

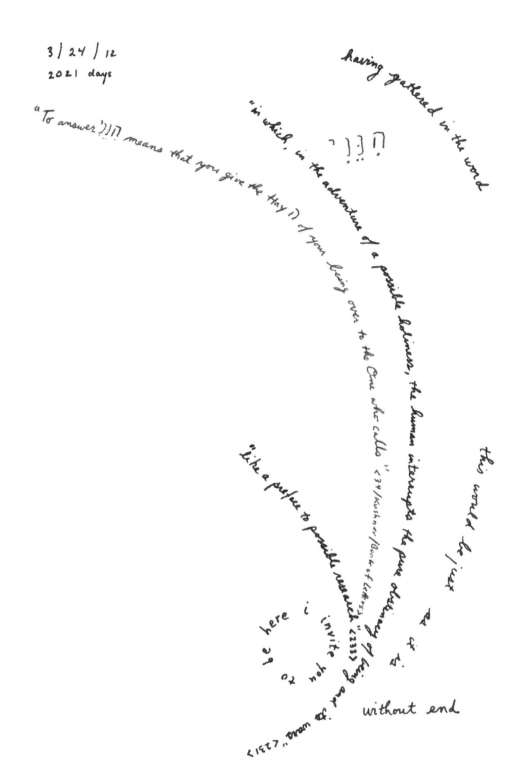

3 / 24 / 12
2021 days

having gathered in the word

"To answer"? ! ! ? means that you give the Way ! ? of your being over to the One who calls" <34/Kushner/Book of Letters>

" ? ! ? ! ? "

"in which, in the adventure of a possible holiness, the human interrupts the pure obstinacy of being and its war." <231>

"like a preface to possible research" <233>

this would be / is as it is

here i invite you to be

without end

Afterword

Re-reading *N20* is so odd – as I rediscover what and where I was, which is not exactly what and where I am now. Perhaps most surprising – it's only been a little more than six years since I wrote *N20* – I am fully aware that I could not write in the same way now. I return to these pages with a sense of wonder: I wrote this? Merleau-Ponty writes that "a writer hardly ever rereads his own works;" perhaps that is true because we have absorbed and fully internalized what that phase of writing had to give us? Or, perhaps it is because we fear how we will respond to that return to the page? In this case, I did find the return to be quite engaging and illuminating. As if it were written by another, I learned from these pages.

It seems that I thought that this would be the final notebook – the first ten written within a reading of Heidegger's *Being and Time*, and the next ten notebooks (perhaps a balancing out?) written while reading a number of books by Emmanuel Levinas. (Notebooks 1-10 being H [Heidegger]; 11-20 being L [Levinas]; thus, my own initials, HL.) So, there is in *N20*, particularly at the end, a summing up and a tabulating (for example, with March 3, 2012 noted as day 2000 of writing the Notebooks). *N20* was begun on February 12, 2011, and completed on March 24, 2013 (day 2021 of writing the Notebooks); the notebook itself is 112 pages, page size 5 ½" x 7 ¾", and the book is bound in *koa* wood, a revered and sacred Hawaiian wood (the word *koa* means warrior), and the notebook was given to me by my aunt and uncle (Linda and Stan Goodman) as a 50th birthday present. (It is such a beautiful notebook that it took me more than ten years to work up the nerve to write in it.) The specific Levinas books that I was reading while writing *N20* were *Of God Who Comes to Mind* and *Entre Nous*.

It is a notebook full of major events, some personal/familial in nature, others more generally so – from the death of my father-in-law to my first trip to Cuba, to other travels (London & Edinburgh, the former to read with one of my favorite poets, Fanny Howe), to time spent in LA and Honolulu, to a trip with my son as he began his graduate work in screenwriting at USC, to a reading of Adam Levine's gigantic novel *The Instructions*, to a second trip to Havana in which the government (Cuban) applied pressure which caused us to cancel a scheduled jazz-poetry concert, to the devastating tornado that struck Tuscaloosa killing more than fifty people and destroying large parts of the city and the surrounding countryside.

But *N20* is not a travelogue. It is an odd fusion of various kinds of diaries, journals, and day books, with similar qualities of daily observation, though the Notebooks (not just *N20*) demonstrate a devotion to making manifest intervals of consciousness and occasions of shape-as-momentary-insight. As in some day-books, most pages involve a writing down of engaging quotations from my then ongoing reading of the work of Emmanuel Levinas. It is also most definitely – as with much of Early American Literature – a spiritual journal. What's different, distinctive (in *N20*'s predecessors and successors as well) is the shape-writing: each page as a kind of performance or improvisation (written without drafts). Also, *N20* (and its predecessors and successors) becomes a one-of-a-kind artist's book – where the physical book itself is unique in size, texture, and weight (somewhat different than the version you hold in your hand now). In a punning sense, as an artist's book *N20* is an answer to questions such as to what am I drawn? What am I being drawn into? Part of what I was drawn into was an exploration of the possibilities for an almost daunting density of writing. I worry now (as I did not then) that this density of writing and shapes can be off-putting, with a reader wondering whether she or he really wants to take the time required to disentangle, perform (by choosing a path of reading), and absorb each page. I can only hope that the reading experience for readers of *N20* will be sufficiently rewarding to induce the patience required to sustain attention to a given page.

Perhaps the most painful aspect for me of *N20* is the dawning awareness (see September 2011 pages) of my uncle Stan Goodman's developing cognitive loss. Stan, a former neurosurgeon and Biblical scholar, was tremendously important to my own development as a writer and to my return to a much more substantive dwelling in and questioning of my Jewish identity. His dementia led me to think differently about the nature of being itself – the meaning (within being) of this diminishment of some cherished mental and expressive capacities. As his dementia became more severe, I found myself wondering if there are other ways to locate ourselves in being without placing so much of a priority on intensity of intellect. (This kind of thinking – perhaps Jewish? – a thinking against itself occurs throughout *N20*.)

Perhaps it is witnessing and thinking about Stan's decline that is a major factor in moving *N20* toward an ongoing gratitude for (daily) being. *N20* may be read as an exposition of thinking/writing/consciousness as a kind of grace, an intimacy with being, and very important locations of and for gratitude.

As for the book's title – *Thinking in Jewish* – a tip of the hat to Jonathan Boyarin who wrote a book of the same title (1996, University of Chicago Press). In fact, in preparing this afterword I returned to Boyarin's book and found observations quite pertinent to *N20*, including Boyarin's affirmation of what he refers to as his still-unsettled articulation of his own attachment to the name "Jew" (173) and his observation that "what a Jew writes – particularly in a non-Jewish language – is Jewish and non-Jewish at the same time" (195). Mine is a non-essentialized version of being Jewish and thinking in Jewish. The Notebooks are a way of proceeding that is somewhat destabilized, ambiguous, polyvocal, and multi-textual. Perhaps a scene that took place a number of years ago provides a suitable analogy – several people (David Antin, Marjorie Perloff, and Charles Bernstein) sitting around a table, all talking at once, and all listening attentively to each other.

My own identity (like that of everyone else) is multiple in nature – Jewish, Buddhist, poet, Southerner, white, etc. In this particular notebook, that intersection of Jewish and Buddhist manifests itself (see 5/9/11, for example), as does the particular necessity of a Jewish affirmation in a decidedly Christian Deep South (where I have lived for forty years). I agree wholeheartedly with Boyarin's suggestions that "Jewish identity is indeed marked by a constant tension between self-identification, and identification by and as the Other" (112-113).

Boyarin notes:

> There is a phrase sometimes used, by Lubavitchers, by other Hasidim, and by other Jews primarily engaged in intimate Orthodox communities, to describe themselves. They call themselves yidishe yidn, "Jewish Jews." ... The idea of the yiddisher yid moves beyond the pole of givenness in identity, suggesting that on one hand there are Jews who are Jews because Jewishness is given to them, and on the other hand there are (doubled) Jews who make themselves as Jews. Becoming a Jew involves a self-mak-

ing, a doubling, a supplement to the given genealogy. (174-175)

I think that *N20* – and I am grateful to my uncle Stan Goodman for helping to provoke this investigation – is the writing that is that very doubling and self-making. Born a Jew (in San Jose, California, in 1950), for many years I really did not consider (with any kind of sustained thinking) what that meant or might be. I am definitely not a Jewish Jew in the eyes of an Orthodox Jew; in temple, I would feel more comfortable sitting on the other side of the curtain from them. Here, too, in Tuscaloosa, I remain distant from any institutional practice (though I am a member of the temple). The Jew I am is Talmudic and Midrashic in nature; it is a Jew-writing, one who loves commentary, questions, and who does not trust conclusions and who does not think that the most important conversations have an ending. *N20*, with the help of Abraham Heschel's remarkable book *Sabbath*, marks my ongoing attempt to honor and know and live with the Sabbath and its wonderful ways of making time tangible. And with the illuminating presence of Emmanuel Levinas' writing throughout *N20*, "my" writing remains faithful to "the general Jewish tendency to view citation as more authoritative than originality" (Boyarin, 142). Though I would also note that I learned from Robert Duncan this faith in something other than originality much earlier in my writing life.

Though clearly not exclusively a Jewish perspective or affinity, *N20* explores what it means to be of the book, and of the word. Two pages from the end of *N20* one section of the page states "I have served the book / a scribe / in being & time." The final page, in part, offers a meditation on that crucial Hebrew word *henayni* – "here I am," wondering to whom and to what we make such a declaration, wondering what it is that asks us to do so, and questioning and making manifest what it means to be here. The page itself – in the shape, the phrase, the word – offers itself as a place for a reader to be located (for the time being), just as it was a dwelling place (in a stretched version of the momentary) for the writer. I am more than happy to turn it over to you.

—June 2017
Tuscaloosa, Alabama

Praise for *Thinking in Jewish (N20)*

Thinking in Jewish (N20) is indeed a dense and difficult book, but what important book is after all not a challenge, a true Kabbalistic challenge, commanding us to disentangle difficulty, to deal with density and complexity, variability in unity, as Hank Lazer's N20 does? It is precise, all encompassing, emotionally intellectual, and forged in a state of continuous spirituality: and in its precision and risk of expression and vision a book that conveys the true presence of the poet. Hank Lazer the poet (as far as I am concerned, and within the limits of my own knowledge and capabilities) one of the best.

—José Kozer, recipient of the Pablo Neruda Poetry Prize 2013

"decanter sings," the words flow out on paper, the graphic jellyfish silently calls to prayer, the eye touches the hand that writes, the sneakiest hebrew "shin," a vessel, bears across the sea of white paper the reminder that "no one is identical to himself." this poetry is a craft that unbinds us, invites us to share that "note/book/magic/notebook." thank you.

—Jonathan Boyarin, Director of Jewish Studies at Cornell University & author of *Thinking in Jewish*

Are these poems? How to read them, up, down, sideways, spinning the pages, squinting the eyes or maybe drawing back to gawk at the complex lovely organic hand made shapes, words blurred? Or, what are poems, what is writing, what is reading, thinking, philosophy, living, dying, anyway? Such are the problems, questions, and joys of *Thinking in Jewish*, the latest publication in Hank Lazer's truly astonishing experiment in what he calls "shape writing." It would not surprise me if decades from now contemplatives are using this text for spiritual exercise. It is that wondrously open-ended and inexhaustible.

—Norman Fischer, poet, zen priest, author of *any would be if* and *escape this crazy life of tears*

These words move like water. Emblems impressed fluidly between hand and eye. This book is a visual incantation—between writing and drawing, between meditation and dream, between aliveness and loss. In this delicate luminous work, "each word is a transit transitory door." Nothingness, ephemerality, and sinuous mandalas glow throughout. Enter the pages of these notebooks and you will find yourself entering an intimate contemplative expanse. Breath is inscribed here, like rivulets, paths which lead us into verdant yet invisible traces of interior life.

—Laynie Browne, author of *PRACTICE*

Hank Lazer is an astonishing triple threat. His work is vital to the futures of poetry, the visual arts, and the nature of art in general. No artist today better speaks to the radically dynamic hybrid of image and text he employs. Lazer uses the physical shape of language to still the world and magnify and sanctify its extraordinary linguistic, visual, and felt natures. His work provides the water of life and its shape also—and shape is the backbone of this ongoing process. Lazer's technique is no mere artifice. Much like "lyrics" in space, Lazer establishes the vital bond between form and content toward which life and art aspire. While, like Walter Benjamin, historicizing his writing through abundant source notations, he also projects a sense of unrelentingly ceaseless force. "here I invite you to be here" draws Lazer in a circle near the end of his new book, *N20*, that is as it says, "without end." Nearby he quotes Levinas saying, "like a preface to possible research." Lazer's work not only prefaces research and artistic achievement. He also enables and accomplishes it. Crucial to his practice is a gather[ing] in the word"—the gist or logos that clears and creates. The density of these mental, physical, and spiritual cues "upon the face of logos" form a play of vibrant and enveloping linguistic and pictorial fields. Lazer's art plays between the rippling and interactive biblical "let there," "be," and "light" Lazer evokes.

—Stephen Paul Miller, author of *There's Only One God and You're Not It* and co-editor of *Radical Poetics and Secular Jewish Culture*

In Hank Lazer's *Thinking in Jewish*, Levinasian theology dissolves into zen rumination, spun rumination transforms into startling configuration, and sparkling configuration abets looping thought. This is a practice of daily poetry as sublime flicker.

—Charles Bernstein, author of *Pitch of Poetry*

79953418R00076

Made in the USA
Columbia, SC
11 November 2017